Fly Fishing the North Platte River

© ROD WALINCHUS

FLY FISHING THE

NORTH·PLATTE

R I V E R

An Angler's Guide

ROD WALINCHUS

PRUETT PUBLISHING COMPANY
BOULDER, COLORADO

Printed in the United States
10 9 8 7 6 5 4 3 2 1

Library of Congress Cataloging-in-Publication Data

Walinchus, Rod, 1946–
    Fly fishing the North Platte River : an angler's guide / Rod
Walinchus.
        p.   cm.
    Includes index.
    ISBN 0-87108-834-7 (pb : acid-free)
    1. Fly fishing—Wyoming. 2. Fly fishing—North Platte River.
I. Title.
SH565.W34   1994
799.1'755—dc20   93-32562
                                            CIP

Cover and book design by Jody Chapel, Cover to Cover Design

Contents

Acknowledgments

I would like to thank the following people for their assistance in assembling the information contained within these pages, for without their input this project would have been impossible: Bill Witchers, Wyoming Department of Fish and Game, Casper office; Mike Snigg, Wyoming Department of Fish and Game, Laramie office; Robert A. McDowell and his staff for their work on "Fisheries Management Investigations—A Study of the Upper North Platte River Fishery, Carbon County, Wyoming (1975-1981)"; Ken Kehmeier, Colorado Fish and Game; Bob Smith and Tom Wiersma, Great Rocky Mountain Outfitters.

I would also like to extend my gratitude to:

The Great Divide Flyfishers Chapter of Trout Unlimited, Rawlins, Wyoming. Without their unselfish sharing of information over the years much of the river would still be a mystery to me.

Steve Hays. Without his friendship and companionship the days on the river would have been a little less interesting.

My wife, Evelyn, for putting up with me.

Introduction: The Upper North Platte River

I grew up on a river, I now live on a river, and everything in between involved a river—in my reading, my travels, or my daydreams. I learned to fly fish because of a river. My evolution from a little boy with a cheap old bamboo rod and tinny reel filled with rotten Dacron line, catching sunfish with live crickets or frogs with strips of red cloth, to an adult clad in proper attire with the proper tackle, taking wild trout on insect-matching artificials, was as natural as the transition from acne to beard. I consider a river to be a living organism with the moods of a lover, the power of a beast, the gentleness of a child, and the mystery of the ages. Through fly fishing I can live in close union with it. A symbiotic relationship develops. A river gives up its secrets ever so slowly over the years of fishing it; it teaches the observant and frustrates the inflexible. In return, I give it the respect it deserves and, I hope, some protection through my association with various conservation groups.

A river is relentless in its course to a final destination, only to be slowed or momentarily halted by nature or interference from man, yet it finds a way to reach its end. It is life-bearing, not only to the organisms that live in it, but to the surrounding fauna and flora and man in general. We all depend on a river in some form or another, whether for the food from the crops it irrigates or for the recreation it provides; our lives are richer because of it.

The North Platte River in Wyoming has traditionally been a utilitarian river, providing transportation by serving as an avenue for moving items such as logs and railroad timbers, and by irrigating the fields of ranchers and farmers. It has been and still is a workhorse of a river, and it has been managed and treated as such. It is dammed in many spots along its

1

course to hold back its waters for the water-right owners downstream, parts of it have been diverted through ranchers' meadows to provide hay for their animals, and power is derived from the hydroelectric generators of the dams. It is a river that earns its keep in our society.

Recent times have found the sportsman depending on the North Platte for the recreation it provides and not for the game that once was a mainstay. Not too many years ago, the prevailing wisdom was that rivers were places to harvest and, in essence, rape. We have come to accept now that they are places to be preserved and protected. It has been too late for some of the waters in our country, but, mercifully, the North Platte has been spared. It probably still has its problems, but the efforts of those who are concerned with its preservation are there to insure its continued protection.

The North Platte is born in the high country and finds its way downstream through a variety of landscapes. The scenic mountain vistas of the upper river give way to the bottomland associated with ranching in the area and eventually to the sage-covered settings of the high-desert plains. Boulder-strewn, rapid-filled white-water areas give way to slow meandering currents as the river carves its way on its ancient journey downstream. Dams back it up into almost currentless reservoirs, but still it pulses on. The diversity of land it travels through changes the character of the river and makes it seem like several totally different rivers. A visiting angler, after fishing the upper reaches, would be hard-pressed to recognize it as the same river if he were to find himself on some of the downstream sections. It is a river as diverse as any river can be.

Beginning in the high country of northern Colorado, the North Platte winds its way through about three hundred miles of Wyoming into Nebraska, where it merges with the South Platte River en route to the Missouri River, eventually meeting with the Mississippi and dumping into the Gulf of Mexico.

The river effectively defines the southeast corner of Wyoming, flowing north to Casper then east to the Scottsbluff, Nebraska, area. Of the three hundred miles in Wyoming, about ninety miles are classified by the Wyoming Fish and Game Department as Class I, or Blue Ribbon, waters. These are defined as premium trout waters and fisheries of

national importance. The Trout Stream Classification system weighs various characteristics to calculate a value for a stream's aesthetics, availability, and productivity. These values are then combined to determine a stream's classification. Most of the Blue Ribbon water occurs in the upper reaches of the river as it enters Wyoming, some occurs at the Miracle Mile, and the rest in the Gray Reef area.

There are approximately sixty miles of Class II, or Red Ribbon, water, defined as very good trout waters or fisheries of statewide importance. These sections occur in the Rawlins area and in the area upstream of Casper. The 150 miles of river from its entrance in Wyoming to the town of Casper is the area of most interest to the trout fisherman, and is the crux of this book. The remaining 150 miles from Casper to the river's exit from Wyoming are classified as either Class III, IV, or V waters. These range from important trout waters and fisheries of regional importance to very low production waters, often incapable of sustaining a trout fishery.

A good deal of the Blue Ribbon water is managed as a wild trout fishery, or as a Basic Yield Fishery supported by wild trout with some stocking programs. Other classifications of the river are managed through various stocking programs, some of which are strictly put-and-take. There are a few sections of the river that have some special regulations that limit the size, species, and numbers of fish taken, as well as the manner of taking them. But as a rule, it is not regulated to the point of intrusion.

Wyoming is blessed in the sense that it is sparsely populated, and the problems associated with large populations are generally not encountered. The fisheries have been spared misuse because of the low population. Wyoming has had the opportunity to learn from more densely populated areas' mistakes, and has had the ability to head off problems. Management philosophies have grown with the general conservation philosophies of the average fly fisherman. The state fish and game department has become more open and willing to hear and implement proposals from various fishing organizations and individuals regarding fisheries as long as they are biologically sound. The quality of the fisheries in the state has no doubt improved over the past decade and is on the right track for continued improvement.

This is not to say that Wyoming is not without some problems. Local attitudes still reflect the individualistic approach to fisheries—a protective, isolationist posture is the cause of many problems. Many Wyoming citizens view out-of-state fishermen, special regulations, and some management practices as an invasion of their individual rights. There are problems associated with water usage, especially in low-water years. The dewatering of the river for irrigation purposes is a constant sore spot and a hotbed of controversy, because a good deal of Wyoming's economy depends on agribusiness.

Recreational float trips, whether for fishing or not, that use the river flowing over private land have led to many conflicts between landowners and the boating public. Problems include illegal trespass, littering, damage to private property, fences strung across the river, and floaters being run off of public as well as private land. There have even been reports of boaters being fired upon by landowners or their representatives.

The Wyoming Supreme Court decided in a classic legal case (*Day v. Armstrong*, 1961) the future of recreational boating on the North Platte River in Wyoming. This case became the precedent in cases on other recreational rivers in the West. It was decided that the water flowing over private land is state property and considered public, but the land on the banks and beneath the surface of the river is private property. Although this decision defined what was and was not public, it did not stop the conflicts. Landowners heavily posted their lands, suspended signs over the river, and carefully patrolled their properties to keep boaters from stopping.

Wyoming is still a state where the landowner owns the bottom of the river, and it is therefore illegal to touch land without permission. A floating fisherman may not get out of a boat to fish on private land without the express permission of the landowner. There is no access to the high-water mark. I guess it is, technically speaking, even illegal to anchor a boat in private water without permission.

I can sympathize with both sides of the high-water access problem. As a fisherman, it would be great to be able to traverse the stream to the high-water mark, especially when floating. But as a landowner with a home very near to an access site, the invasion of my privacy by shore fishermen is a real problem at times. I don't know if there ever will be a real solution, especially because all kinds of people are involved. If every fisherman were polite, respectful, and considerate of landowners' rights, and every landowner were open, generous, and aware of a fisherman's needs, then there would not be a problem. Fortunately, there are landowners in Wyoming who will grant permission to the fisherman who takes the time to ask, and, equally fortunately, there are fishermen who respect the rights of landowners and do not intrude on their right to privacy.

There is very good public access to the North Platte River. Almost its entire course can be floated, and there are enough access points along the way to allow the fly fisher to tailor a trip or get out and fish frequently. The shore and wading fisherman will find plenty of public access sites. I suppose that because there is private water we all succumb to the desire to fish it, thinking it probably will be better fishing. But we all know that isn't necessarily the case; it's kind of like wanting the candy that Mom has hidden from you.

The character of the North Platte depends on what part of the river you happen to be on. It can be a classic western free-flowing river susceptible to the whims of Mother Nature, or a tailwater with fishable water open all year. The upper river is classic, with spectacular views in unpopulated areas. The wild trout fishery of this area only enhances the experience one can have here. Wild trout can be unbelievably easy to catch one day and frustratingly difficult the next. Management practices have turned this part of the river into a total wild trout fishery with over four thousand fish per mile. There are not too many places in the country where an angler can fish a river such as this and do it without fighting crowds.

The tailwater sections of the river have wild trout supported by stocked species. Both the Miracle Mile and Gray Reef tailwaters are trophy fisheries, and many fish caught there weigh in the teens.

The water in the North Platte, especially in the upper reaches, is slightly tea-colored. Because of this stained water I have heard people talk of the fish there as "clear fish." These are fish that are difficult to see in the water. Those of you who like to sight-fish to resting fish or fish feeding on the bottom will find seeing fish in the upper river difficult. Often I hear people complaining while they float the river that they can't see fish, so there mustn't be too many around. Obviously, this is not the case. Sometimes the tailwaters, especially when they are very low, are gin-clear. Fishing in these conditions requires all the technical expertise an angler can muster. Mostly, the fish in these waters are underfished and certainly underpressured. They have not been beaten to death as on some western spring creeks; they will reward a semicompetent angler.

With over three hundred miles of river to write about, it should be evident that no one person can comprehensively cover the entire North Platte River and what happens on it. There will be omissions that some who have intimate knowledge of particular sections will notice. The intent of this book is to provide a relatively accurate and detailed information source for the fly fisherman—a definitive book on this river would be volumes long and impractical to the angler. What I hope to accomplish is to give an average angler an understanding of the river in general, its insect life, and the angling techniques to use on it, so that he or she can make an informed decision about where, when, and how to take a fish or two.

1

The History of the North Platte River as a Fishery

The North Platte River today is nationally important as a trout fishery, the quality of which attracts anglers from all over the country. However, there was a time when there weren't any trout in the river. It's hard to imagine this great river without any trout, particularly because in some ways trout are symbolic of the quality of life. Whether trout are important for actually sustaining life, vitalizing an economy, or simply as a recreational pastime matters little—they have become extremely important as a resource. Not to have trout is not to have a way of life.

The rainbow, brown, cutthroat, and brook trouts are not indigenous to the North Platte River drainage. Species that are include a variety of suckers, sauger, chubs, dace, and darters. Trout were introduced to the river along with walleye, an assortment of baitfish, and carp. Documentation of the initial introductions of trout to the upper river is sketchy, but it is assumed that the first recorded introductions must have been made between 1879 and 1882. There are records of approximately fifty thousand rainbow and brook trout planted in tributary streams to the North Platte. They were shipped in barrels from Wisconsin in 1880, when Wyoming was still a territory. In 1879, the first territorial fish commissioner was appointed and most likely oversaw this attempt at stocking the drainage. Then, in 1882, a Board of Fish Commissioners was formed, and its responsibilities included the propagation, cultivation, and protection of food fishes in the waters of Wyoming Territory. The year 1882 was devoted almost entirely to the planting of "native" trout and other varieties in the river. "Native" apparently meant trout species that were native to the United States. Brook trout and "salmon trout" (rainbow trout) were placed into the river at Fort Steele in 1882.

The Board of Fish Commissioners recommended carp for general introduction to all areas. In 1883 they received their first shipment of 560 "minor" carp and distributed them to "applicants." The board extolled the virtues of carp as a ranchman's fish, saying carp are to fishes what chickens are to birds. They then went on to emphasize protecting carp from predacious fish.

In 1881, all accessible streams and lakes in Albany, Carbon, and Laramie counties were stocked with rainbow and brook trout that were shipped from other states. There were no trout hatcheries in the territory until 1884. Some areas were also stocked with largemouth bass and sunfish, but these fish failed to thrive due to unsuitable habitat. Brown trout were distributed into the river from the state fish hatchery at Soldier Springs near Laramie as early as 1890.

By 1890, most of the upper river had been fairly well stocked with fish that were raised and distributed from the hatchery at Soldier Springs. These fish included cutthroat, brook, steelhead, brown, and rainbow trout, plus an experimental planting of grayling. The North Platte was stocked, as were tributary streams like Brush Creek, Cow Creek, Encampment River, South Spring Creek, and Jack Creek. The Union Pacific Railroad served as the principal means of transporting these fish, and the railroad bridge near Fort Steele was probably the distribution point. Here fish were hauled to other areas, most likely on horseback or by wagon.

In 1915, the Saratoga National Fish Hatchery was built for the purpose of producing fingerling trout. It was a federal hatchery, and from 1915 to 1964 was the source of most of the trout stocked into the upper North Platte drainage. Since that time, most planted fish have come from the Wyoming Department of Fish and Game hatcheries and rearing stations. But up until 1977, the Saratoga National Hatchery would dump annual culls from their rainbow brood stock into the river. This hatchery is now mainly responsible for stocking some waters on national forest lands and the Wind River Indian Reservation.

Since 1915, various trout species have been stocked in ever-changing amounts. Rainbow, brown, brook, and cutthroat trout were all stocked, but the brook and cutthroat trout have not played a significant role in stocking for over fifty years. Brook trout plantings have largely been confined to tributaries, and the species was last planted in the river in 1969. Brown trout were deleted from stocking programs in 1969 because their populations were largely self-sustaining, but the program was later continued. Large spotted cutthroat varieties were stocked in the early to mid-1940s and probably interbreed with wild rainbow trout, causing the cuttbow hybrid phenomena. Pure strains of cutthroat are now a rarity in the river. The cutthroat and brook trout originally planted in the river never seemed to establish themselves well, and rainbow and brown trout make up the majority of the fish in the river. However, brook trout have done exceptionally well in the North Platte's tributaries.

The upper river has seen private stockings of trout. The A Bar A Ranch has been authorized to plant catchable-size rainbows in its section of the river and in Big Creek since 1964, although it has not stocked the river since 1984. The "Ryan Renegade Club" was allowed to plant rainbow fingerlings on the Cecil Ryan Ranch between 1964 and 1977. Storer Ranches built a private fish hatchery that would later become the source of private stocking by the Old Baldy Club. This stocking was limited to club property, which contained a number of enclosed reservoirs. Plants directly into the river were not authorized, but stock was occasionally planted in a side channel that ran through the property and found its way into the main river. In 1980, the hatchery ceased operations for production. However, the brood ponds are still intact and provide large rainbows for club use.

Federal water development in the Platte Basin brought about the first major impoundment on the river in the form of Pathfinder Dam, completed in 1911. Seminoe, the most upstream reservoir on the river, was completed in 1939. Around 1953, other major water-development projects upstream of Seminoe were proposed. These included the possibility of dam sites near Douglas Creek, Bennett Peak, and Fort Steele. These proposed developments were judged to be detrimental to the existing natural resource values of the river and have apparently been eliminated from further consideration.

Walleye have never been officially introduced into Seminoe Reservoir or the river above it, yet they are there in growing numbers. Several theories have attempted to explain their introduction. One theory is that in the 1950s a private pond containing walleye that was located in Colorado near the North Platte's headwaters washed out. These fish entered the North Platte River and drifted down to Seminoe Reservoir because the habitat upstream was not suitable. Another theory contends that walleye entered the reservoir by way of the Medicine Bow River, a tributary draining into the reservoir. (Como Bluff hatchery handled walleye eggs in the late 1950s and early 1960s and is located on Rock Creek, which flows into the Medicine Bow River.) No matter how these fish got into the river system, they are definitely there and steadily increasing in numbers. They have been found as far upstream as the state line. Walleye can be found in the river between the months of April and late August, and although they are not a serious problem now, they are a potential threat to the river's trout fishery.

Fishing regulations have changed dramatically since 1900, when an angler was permitted to keep twenty pounds of gamefish, none of which could be a trout or bass less than six inches in length per day. The season lasted from May through October. I guess one had to accurately estimate weight or carry a scale. The regulations also prohibited the removal of fish from waters that were newly stocked for two years. By 1936, the season ran from April 1 through November 30 and allowed an angler to take twenty fish or fifteen pounds per day with no minimum size limitation. As the years progressed, the regulations changed. In 1951 and 1952 the regulations stated one could take fourteen pounds and one gamefish, not to exceed twelve fish on Forest, and ten pounds and one gamefish, not to exceed ten fish off Forest, during the May 15 through October 15 season. Fishing was open year-round in 1969, and the daily limit was eight pounds and one gamefish, not to exceed ten fish. The 1974-75 regulations did away with fishing with live baitfish upstream of Interstate 80, largely at the request of landowners, fishermen, and outfitters who felt that the use of live baitfish was causing an overharvest of trout and an unfair advantage for boat fishermen. The creel limit in 1976 was reduced to six fish per day with no weight limit. In 1982, six trout per day with only one over twenty inches plus ten brook trout under eight inches was the rule, and this is still the general statewide regulation. However, there are numerous sections of the river where these regulations may change on a yearly basis.

The year 1982 also brought special regulations to the upper river from Saratoga to the state line. A slot limit went into effect, making it mandatory to release all fish in the slot. The regulation states six trout per day, only one of which may exceed sixteen inches, and all between

ten and sixteen inches must be released. Angling is by artificial flies and lures only.

The liberal limits and restrictive seasons of the early years have given way to liberal seasons and restrictive limits. This is most likely a reflection of the change in philosophy and attitude of the general fishing public. The catch-and-release promotion by various trout conservation organizations has changed the thinking of a great many sportsmen over the years.

N

1 2 3 4 5

125

Routt Launch Site

127

COWDREY

Canadian River

Michigan River

NORTH PLATTE RIVER

North Fork

125

WALDEN

Roaring Fork

14

125

Little Grizzly Creek

Grizzly Creek

2

The Headwaters

Every river has to begin somewhere. The North Platte begins in the North Park region of northern Colorado at the confluence of Grizzly and Little Grizzly creeks, about forty miles south of the Wyoming-Colorado border near Walden. This river doesn't actually begin as some tiny stream in the high country: its birth occurs in a rangeland environment. A name change is all that defines it as a separate entity where the two creeks meet. A short distance downstream, other creeks such as Roaring Fork, North Fork, the Michigan River, and the Canadian River all add their water to the North Platte. What starts as a relatively slow, meandering, meadowlike river soon changes character as it begins to drop in elevation down a steep gradient at the Northgate Canyon area near the Wyoming state line. The Windy Hole rapids are a little more than a half-mile from the Routt launch site, and, depending on the water conditions, can be rated from Class 4 rapids (medium difficulty, some maneuvering necessary; low ledges, slow rock gardens, medium-regular waves) to Class 7 rapids (long rapids, waves powerful and irregular; dangerous rocks, boiling eddies, inspection usually necessary; powerful and precise maneuvering required; maximum safety precautions necessary). The river becomes so formidable that when the flows reach twenty-nine hundred cubic feet per second, paddle boats, kayaks, and canoes are prohibited.

This turbulent water is at the downstream section of this portion of the river. Most of the North Platte that flows through Colorado isn't so dramatic but is a kinder, gentler kind of water. When the flows are low, an angler has to use stealth as part of his presentation, keeping his body low so it is not silhouetted against the sky. This headwaters section of stream is basically two types of river: the upper portion is a slow meandering meadow-type river, and the last portion is a turbulent, rip-roaring river. This makes the fisheries totally different, and because the water that is characteristic of Northgate is in essence the same as that of most of the upper stretch in Wyoming, this chapter will discuss the slower waters.

Topography

The headwaters of the North Platte River originate in a rangeland environment. This isn't to say that the elevation isn't high: It is 8,200 feet. Mountains surround this area and present an astonishing view when they are snowcapped. The tributaries that rush to fill the North Platte originate, for the most part, in the alpine regions. At these elevations, fall comes early and spring comes late, making for a narrower slot of time in which to fish. This area is responsible for a good deal of the water in the river, and many of the folks who fish the river in Wyoming keep an eye on the snowpack here and in the surrounding mountains. Snowpack measurements are taken and published in the local newspapers, along with forecasts for water levels. This information is important to the people who depend on the river to irrigate their hay fields or crops, as well as to the people who use the river for recreation.

Water Characteristics

Slow-moving, flattish water best typifies this section of the river. It is lined with willows and brush that often make casting to a rising fish a nightmare. There are some riffles and pools but nothing spectacular—it reminds me of Slough Creek in Yellowstone National Park. The river meanders through the rangeland, twisting and turning through its downstream journey. Because it is slow, the bottom in many places here is very silty and offers little cover for the trout. Throughout a good portion of the season when it isn't frozen, the river carries a fair amount of sediment, making it a bit murky.

I would guess this is the first section of the North Platte that is susceptible to dewatering by irrigators. The surrounding ranching communities need the water from the river to grow their crops and to provide grass for their cattle. They become the first of many to draw water from the North Platte to use for irrigation. This poses some problems to the fisherman and to the river itself. Water levels are up during runoff and then get drawn to a mere trickle during the irrigating season; cover that was great for trout becomes high and dry when the flows are low. The fish are forced to hold in less-than-ideal locations. The fisherman will find superior fishing for only a relatively brief period of time during the season when the water is somewhere near normal flows. A major problem for the float fisherman is that he needs high water to float effectively, but it also needs to be clear enough to fish. This set of circumstances doesn't occur on a regular basis throughout the summer. The high runoff water is generally too dirty to fish, and then the irrigators begin pulling water from the river.

A popular float is from the upstream meadow section near Cowdrey to the Routt launch site near the entrance to Windy Hole Rapids. This can be an iffy float because the Canadian River tributary is noted for its propensity to dirty the North Platte. An angler driving from some distance away (everywhere is some distance away out here) may find conditions to be unsatisfactory when he arrives. The fishing can be quite good on this stretch, so it warrants the effort, but more often than not the trip will be less than ideal.

It seems that on every stretch of river there is one tributary that makes life miserable for the traveling fisherman. A strong early-summer rain will also muck up this section of river. The good news is that there are some nearby stillwaters that can offer some great fishing: North, South, and East Delaney lakes hold some good fish, as does Lake John. It should also be mentioned that the Michigan River will offer the trout fisherman some action. It is smaller than the North Platte but does have more character and better holding water.

Accessibility

Accessibility is a problem on this stretch of river, because most of it flows through private property. There are some lease agreements with several of the ranchers in the area, but these seem to be in a state of flux. The state has recently lost several leases, so a discussion of individual leases may be moot by the time you read this. Check with the

The river upstream of the Routt Access.

Colorado Department of Fish and Game, or stop into one of the stores that sell fishing supplies in Walden for more accurate information. The leases that are still available are usually posted, so the shy angler can drive around and find water to fish. The Routt launch site is a public access facility where an angler can follow a trail to find some fishable water.

Whenever you do find yourself fishing water on a lease, remember that the state doesn't own the land—it is privately held. Treat it as if it were your own and respect the rights of the landowner, then maybe other leases will not be lost. "Abuse it and lose it" would be my way of thinking if I were a landowner. It is unfortunate that leases have been lost, but we can take precautions to prevent the loss of others.

Management Practices

The limited amount of access to the river here plays a part in the management of this section. A goal of the Colorado Department of Fish and Game is to establish natural reproduction of rainbow trout. Currently, the department does plant catchable (five-inch fish) rainbows that are hatchery fish and a wild strain in the headwaters. The problem is that they only do it at two locations west of Walden, one of which is the Verner-Brownlee lease. After talking to the department, I get the feeling that if accessibility were better, more of an effort would be made to establish these rainbows. As it now stands, the department hopes to get the rainbows going with limited plantings and that over time enough will survive to begin reproducing naturally.

Thirty-five percent of the fish in this section of the river are rainbows, and the remaining sixty-five percent are brown trout. The brown trout are self-sustaining, so they are managed as wild trout, with no supplemental stockings. The brown trout in this section of river have been referred to as "piggy" browns, the kind that resemble little footballs. The slower water of a meadow stream lends itself to the lifestyle of the brown trout. The temperatures get relatively high in late summer, and browns can adapt and tolerate them better than can other species of trout. Browns seem to be able to sustain themselves better than other trout do.

Farther on downstream, at the entrance to Northgate Canyon, the fishery is managed as a totally wild trout fishery. This is Gold Medal water, Colorado's highest classification of trout water. This section immediately flows into the Blue Ribbon (Wyoming's highest classification of trout water) section of river in Wyoming, which is also managed as a wild trout fishery.

The opportunity to catch wild fish has always appealed to me, and especially so because I spent a good deal of my childhood years in New Jersey. There, much of the trout fishing was strictly put-and-take. Thank the fishing gods that management practices have changed for the better. Compared to that period and place, fishing in the canyon section of the North Platte's headwaters is the opposite end of the spectrum. Here an angler can fish in relative solitude and catch wild fish; this is a possible candidate for fly fisher heaven.

Seasonal Changes in Fishing

At the river's elevation of over 8,000 feet here, the window of opportunity to experience good fishing is shorter than at lower elevations. The snows and freezing weather tend to linger a little longer in the spring and return a little earlier in the fall. Obviously, winter puts this section of water under a frozen blanket of snow, without any opportunities for the fisherman. The early spring is marked by runoff. Summer brings the fly fisherman his best shot at finding the river here cooperative. Fall finds the water at severely low levels that are detrimental to good fishing. Unfortunately, the summertime window of opportunity gets even smaller because of irrigation needs.

Spring (March, April, and May)

March is a difficult month to endure. There are years when the headwaters of the river will still be in the clutches of winter during March. The spring months are important for the moisture they bring to the river, especially so if there has not been much of an accumulation of snow over the winter months. The droughtlike conditions of the early 1990s has brought a below-average snowpack that spells trouble for the river. If it weren't for the moisture of the spring, the entire river would be in dire straits.

If the river isn't frozen, runoff will start in these months. Neither of these conditions are conducive to good fishing, and the spring rains and snows will only add to the tumult. On occasion, there may be a brief period of clear water before runoff starts in full force. If a fisherman can hit it right, he could sneak in some early-season fishing. The water will be cold and the fish lethargic, but some general attractor-style nymphs just might produce some of these fish. This is obviously a hit-or-miss proposition.

As the spring months wear on and the runoff waters begin to abate, the water clears. The flows are still on the high side, but the clearing water makes things fishable and certainly floatable. This occurs sometime in May during normal years and signals the beginning of the window of opportunity to the fisherman.

Early Summer

The early part of the summer, usually in late May and June, offers the angler the best chance for good fishing. Conditions are as ideal for this section as they can be: good flows that are relatively clear. It should be remembered that this portion of the North Platte carries a heavy sediment load under normal conditions, so exceptionally clear water will not usually be found. But the water will be clear enough to fish.

The combination of high flows and clearish water makes it floatable, which opens up more water to the fisherman. Floating can give the angler a chance at fishing places that are normally inaccessible. The higher water provides the trout with more areas for cover along banks that are high and dry later in the year. The fish will move to cover along the banks, and the float fisherman will have an easier time simply because he can present his offerings to them without interference from streamside vegetation. A wading fisherman can usually work over an area more thoroughly than a float fisherman, but the float fisherman will work over more fish in the course of a day, so things do balance out.

At this time of year the float fisherman will find good action using general patterns like Woolly Buggers and Bitch Creeks. A friend of mine does well with a cranefly larva pattern that he fishes somewhat like a streamer. He will cast to the bank and let it swing with the current or strip it back to the boat. These patterns are generally fished with a sinking-tip line or are heavily weighted. Anglers with a floating line can weight the patterns or the leader by adding enough split shot to get the imitation down near the bottom quickly. Fish the pockets and cover along the bank by casting as close as possible to the bank, and either begin stripping the line back immediately or do nothing and let the boat pull the imitation away from the bank. Strikes will usually occur within a foot or two of the bank. Many times a fish will hit the imitation as soon as it hits the water.

The month of June is the peak time for insect hatches on this section of river. The most abundant insect is the caddis, which usually hatches around late morning. Finding a riffle with hatching caddis can best be accomplished by the float fisherman, but a walking fisherman with a working knowledge of the river, or one that gets a break, can experience some good dry-fly action. I usually like a caddis hatch because I don't have to be technical in my presentations. If the fly drags a bit, so what—caddisflies usually skid around on the surface anyway, and if I let my pattern swing in the current it may even imitate an emerging pupa's actions.

The traditional wet-fly fisherman will find plenty of accommodating fish during a caddis hatch. An Elk Hair Caddis in a #14 will be more than adequate at this time of year. A few emergent caddis patterns or soft hackles and a handful of caddis larva patterns should round out the arsenal.

An angler can also expect to find some mayflies hatching in June. The most common are probably *Baetis* species, little blue-winged olives, and *Rhithrogena* species, commonly called the western march brown. *Baetis* usually hatch out in the late morning, around the time the caddis hatch. Finding fish feeding on these small mayflies is a matter of looking in the right places. The caddis are normally in the riffles, and fish feeding on them can best be identified by the splashy or showy riseforms. Fish feeding on *Baetis* will normally be found in calmer water, and the rise-forms will be much more subtle. Look downstream of a riffle along the banks for fish feeding on *Baetis* duns, or along the quieter edges of the riffles.

Prior to the hatch, a fisherman can nymph-fish with small pheasant-tail nymphs and have good success. During the hatch any #18 mayfly adult pattern will usually work, but the patterns that specifically imitate these tiny olive mayflies will probably take more fish. I have caught my share of fish with a small Adams during one of these hatches. These fish have not been hammered to the point where an angler has to have no-hackle-type imitations to fool highly selective fish.

Later in the afternoon or evening, one can expect to see small hatches of the western march brown. These are relatively large mayflies

The river in North Park.

that can be matched on a #10 hook. They have mottled brown wings and a two-tone body. The back is a reddish brown, and the undersides are usually a lighter brown, tan, or have an olive cast. Fishing the dun stage is best when the weather is on the cool side, because the insect will stay on the surface for a longer drift, making it more available to the trout. If the weather is warm, the duns will fly off rather quickly. The nymphs of this species emerge by rapidly rising to the surface, much like many caddis emergers. A soft-hackled pattern fished with a classic wet-fly down-and-across swing can be deadly. Nymph-fishing with Hare's Ear patterns can also be good, especially if the fly is allowed to swing with the current at the end of the drift.

During this time of year, an angler can have very good fishing for fat, healthy brown trout and the occasional rainbow. If he is lucky enough to be in the right places at the right times, he may even be able to spend most of the day fishing to rising fish with dry flies. The floating fisherman will have a better opportunity to get in on some of these hatches because he can cover more water and find pods of feeding fish. The time between periods of rising fish can be filled by nymph-fishing. A variety of mayfly nymphs, caddis larvae, and even some stonefly nymphs are available for the angler to imitate.

Midsummer to Fall

By the middle of July, the irrigators have drawn the river down to a mere trickle. This messes up the good fishing. Some of the water used for irrigation eventually returns to the river but brings two problems with it: High nutrient loads are common in returning water because it has flowed through fertilized fields, and the temperature of the water has increased to a point that is marginally unhealthy for the fish. The increase in temperature is the culprit that puts the fishing off for the rest of the summer. The fish are reluctant to feed heavily when the temperatures are high, so an angler can cover water where just a few weeks ago he had super fishing and swear that there isn't a fish left in the river.

These low flows with high temperatures continue until the irrigation season is over. By that time, the temperatures remain on the high side anyway. Fall will find water temperatures starting to cool somewhat, but the water level remains low, and that is detrimental to fall fishing. It should be noted that the fishing during the fall months is excellent in the Gold Medal section at the Northgate Canyon area. Apparently there are enough tributaries that flow into the river there, so even though the levels may be low, the temperatures are normal.

There is a short season on this stretch of river primarily because mankind has interfered with the river. If left alone, the fishing would probably be good for most of the spring, summer, and fall months. I suppose we should be thankful for the fishing that exists and simply go somewhere else when things get bad.

Locally Effective Patterns

Western March Brown Soft-Hackle

Hook: 10-16
Thread: Brown
Tail: Pheasant-tail fibers
Body: Dark brown hare's ear
Hackle: Brown partridge

Western March Brown

Hook: 10-14
Thread: Tan
Wings: Wood duck flank fibers
Tails: Brown hackle fibers
Body: Tan hare's ear
Hackle: Grizzly and brown, mixed

Other Effective Patterns

Adams
Elk Hair Caddis
Humpies
Little Blue-Winged Olive
Blue Dun
Trudes
Woolly Buggers
Halfbacks
Prince Nymph
Gold-Ribbed Hare's Ear
Pheasant-Tail Nymph
Bitch Creek
Cranefly larva

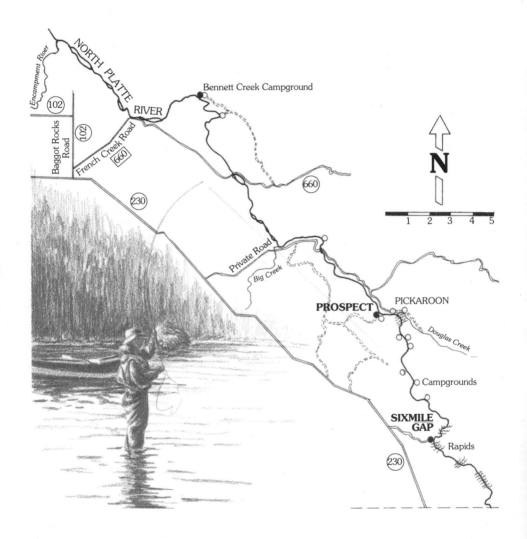

Encampment River

NORTH PLATTE

RIVER

Bennett Creek Campground

(102)

Baggot Rocks Road

French Creek Road

(102)

(660)

(230)

(660)

N

1 2 3 4 5

Private Road

Big Creek

PROSPECT PICKAROON

Douglas Creek

Campgrounds

SIXMILE
GAP

Rapids

(230)

3

The Headwaters
to the Encampment River

This is perhaps the most majestic section of the entire river because it flows through Wyoming's Medicine Bow National Forest. Access is a problem, for a good deal of this upper river is in the Platte River Wilderness Area. At various times in the past this part of the river and its corridor have been recommended for study under the Wild and Scenic Rivers Act. The scenery is as breathtaking as one will find anywhere in the country, and for that reason alone it is worth a visit. Of course, great fishing helps, and this section of water certainly has that. Combine the magnificent vistas with fantastic fishing, then add very few people to the recipe and a fisherman's fantasy comes to life. This is the upper North Platte River.

This is a wild fishery in every sense of the word. An angler can catch totally wild rainbows and brown trout in this rugged setting and see elk, deer, bears, Big Horn sheep, bobcats, mountain lions, coyotes, bald eagles, and even an occasional moose in the process. People who like to get away from it all will find this area a delight: It is one of the most underfished sections of the entire river. The ruggedness might play a part, but because this section of the river lies in a very sparsely populated area and is a fairly long drive from everywhere, it gets very little pressure. There are localized sections of river that have decent fishing and are easier to access, so they get the brunt of the fishermen. But this section seems to be reserved for people who have a few days to spend and want a wilderness experience.

During the early part of the season, at the tail end of the runoff, a fair amount of people like to raft the white-water sections for the thrill of it. If the water cooperates, some of these people might bring along a

Float-fishing the banks.

fishing rod, but the emphasis is on the excitement of the float. The rapid-filled section is confined to the first eighteen or so miles from the Routt launch site in Colorado.

After the white-water season is over, a few of the locals will float-fish this upper section until the water levels begin to drop. The fishing is superb, the scenery exhilarating, and it is worth every bit of the difficulty of getting a boat to the water. As the water levels begin to drop, these float fishermen move farther on downstream to do their fishing because it becomes difficult to maneuver a boat in this shallow, rock-strewn section of river.

Topography

On the North Platte's thirty-seven-or-so-mile journey from the Colorado state line to the mouth of the Encampment River, it flows through some varied country. The upper section lies in the forested mountains of the Medicine Bow National Forest and can be characterized as canyonlike. Steep grades are dominant elements of the landscape, accounting for the proliferation of white-water areas. One will generally find oneself walking down to the water in this section. In this forested area the typical vegetation will include such species as Engelmann spruce, Douglas fir, subalpine fir, ponderosa pine, limber pine, and lodgepole pine. There are also cedar and aspen intermixed with lower-story species such as willows, grasses, and sagebrush.

As the river leaves the forest, the terrain changes to a more rolling section, much like a foothill area. It begins a slight meandering as it flows through sparsely populated ranching land. The riparian vegetation along the agricultural lands includes occasional conifers such as ponderosa and limber pines, cedar, aspen, and cottonwood. The understory will include dense willows, chokecherry, wild rose, and a variety of grasses. At Bennett Peak the river once again flows through a canyonlike environment, but the vegetation remains consistent with this lower area.

Water Characteristics

The term "white water" brings to mind steep gradients, narrow canyons, and numerous very large boulders scattered throughout the water. This is the upper portion of this section of river. It is the only section of the approximately three hundred miles of the North Platte flowing through Wyoming where there is any form of rapids. The boulders and rocks scattered about the river create an abundant instream fish habitat. Deep pools are gouged into the river and provide holding areas for trout, especially when water levels drop.

As one moves downstream out of the white-water areas, the river begins to meander a little more and small instream islands increase in number. The islands add to the overall character of the water. Currents of varying speeds meet at the ends of islands, creating super feeding habitat for trout. The riffles-to-pools ratio is excellent in this stretch, and there are plenty of instream rocks to provide holding areas for fish. As water levels begin to drop, these rocks become navigational hazards that keep the oarsman on his toes. This is a section of river where it pays to float with friends who know how to row, especially if they're in your boat. The water here is relatively shallow and reminds me of the Madison River—one very long riffle. There are numerous pockets behind rocks, along some banks, and on the downstream side of small islands that provide good trout habitat.

A great deal of the tributary streams are present in this stretch of river. These tributaries, when combined with the steep gradient of the river itself, offer better water clarity than in other sections of the river, and more trout spawning and nursery habitat. It appears that very few of the tributaries in this section are the kind that roil the main river at the first sign of bad weather.

The bottom of the river here is mostly comprised of rocky rubble. Car-sized boulders can be found here, along with pea-sized gravel and everything in between. It does seem like most of the river bottom is made up of rocks large enough to trip over or slide off. Whenever I get the opportunity to wade this section, I spend a fair amount of time trying to get dry. An angler can get by with hip boots in the summer, but if he is anything like me he'll always wade over the tops of the boots.

Farther downstream in the Bennett Peak area, the river once again goes through a canyon environment. The characteristics of the water here are deep pools and many large boulders instream. A number of the deep pools are along the banks. This type of water obviously is good trout habitat and great spots to toss a Woolly Bugger into when float-fishing. Because this upper section of river is free-flowing, the water provides the variety of trout habitat that has enabled wild trout to prosper and flourish.

Accessibility

The good news is that there is plenty of public land on this section, especially in the upper national forest portion. The bad news is that there are very few points from which to access it. As a matter of fact, there is no paved road along this entire stretch that leads to the river. The best roads one can expect to travel that actually go near the river are gravel, which the Wyoming Fish and Game Department refers to as "All Weather Roads" on their access map (someone there has an odd sense of humor). Most of the roads that lead to the water's edge are referred to as "Primitive Roads," which is a more accurate description.

Hikers, campers, backpackers, and the wade fisherman will find the best access, especially those willing to walk a distance. There is an eight-and-a-half-mile foot trail from the Sixmile Gap access that runs along the river all the way to the Pickaroon access through the wilderness area. There are nine or ten actual campsites along the trail for fishermen wanting to take time and spend a few days in relative isolation. Sixmile is an easy place to reach because a paved road from Saratoga in Wyoming and from Walden in Colorado runs fairly close to it. The drive is scenic with very little traffic.

Pickaroon, on the other hand, is not an easy place to reach. The road is a decent gravel road, at least until it nears the river, but it's a long way from anywhere. No matter which direction one comes from— Saratoga, Walden, or Laramie—a fair amount of time will be consumed just getting to it. Obviously, these are strictly summertime accesses.

The float fisherman will find these upper accesses tough to deal with. In order to put a boat in at Sixmile, one must drag or carry it down a fairly steep slope for about a quarter of a mile. This is not an access for anglers with drift boats; canoes, rafts, or other light craft are better suited to the portage. Pickaroon is easier on the drift boat owner because the boat can be trailered right to the river, although there is no ramp. A low spot in the bank is the best that can be hoped for. Getting the boat in the river will require a little work, which is no big deal, but the shuttle will take hours to accomplish. So, this is not a practical access for the float fisherman.

Just downstream of Pickaroon on the west side of the river is a more practical access—sort of—called Prospect. Shuttles will be shorter to the access points downstream, but the road in is so bad that even four-wheel-drives will find it impassable at times. There is a very steep, badly eroded grade down to the river. When it is dry it's traversable, but barely, and when it is the least bit wet it's impossible, unless one enjoys sliding down a hillside in his vehicle. This is an access to be used during good, dry weather with four-wheel-drive and a fair amount of time to give to a shuttle.

A few of the fishing shops in Saratoga will provide shuttle services to anglers. Stop by and visit to learn more. Since shuttles can take large amounts of time, often as much as two hours, it may be worthwhile to have someone else make them, whatever the price.

About eight more miles down the river is another one of those impractical access points, Big Creek. It sits on public land but cannot be reached from the west side of the river, where the road is good. To reach the site from the east side of the river, a trek through the forest is required with a fair amount of travel on primitive roads. The department of fish and game and the BLM are looking into making this site a viable access sometime in the future.

The next access site is the Bennett Peak Campground and Corral Creek camping area, about nine and a half more miles downstream. On a map it appears as a convenient access area—not too far from Saratoga, about twelve miles from the next take-out, and still far enough upstream to attract a few people. The problem is that there is no direct way to get to it. From both sides of the river one must take French Creek Road, a decent gravel road, way past the access, then travel on a primitive road back to the area. This is time-consuming. The launch area is nothing more than a low sandy spot in the bank where a two-wheel-drive vehicle could easily get stuck.

Once the river leaves the national forest, it enters areas of private land. The float fisherman will be confined to the boat in these sections. There are small public parcels scattered throughout the private sectors. The Great Divide Flyfishers, a club from Rawlins, has created signs on the river as part of a three-year cooperative effort with the BLM to identify public access. The signs are small blue or red rectangles: red signifies private land and blue public. The signs enable the float fisherman to identify where he can legally get out of the boat to fish or rest without trespassing. Because the access areas are so far apart and hard to reach, many anglers attempt to use private sections and find themselves charged with trespass violations. These small signs might prevent that from happening.

Accessibility to this section of river seems to be tailored to the walk fisherman who has some time to spend in the area and doesn't mind camping at primitive sites. Many of the local anglers spend most of their time floating the lower sections of river. Although I really enjoy floating this stretch of river, I only manage a few trips a year. It is simply more convenient for me to take a few days to camp and walk than it is to attempt to float these sections in one day. Many people will bring camping gear in their boats and take a couple of days to do this section. This is a more sensible approach to float-fishing the upper river. I suppose the poor access is an even trade-off for the relative isolation and stunning beauty the area offers.

Management Practices

Wyoming is a state with relatively few people for its size. There was a time during the energy boom of the 1970s and early 1980s when it seemed that Wyoming would experience a huge population surge. There was a good deal of money to be made here, and people began flocking to the state. The boom has turned to bust in most of the state, and population levels are decreasing, with the exception of a few areas that were never dependent on the energy industry. Most of the south-central section of the state had its economy tied to energy.

The large influx of people into the state during the boom had the department of fish and game concerned about how it would impact the fisheries; they anticipated an increase in fishing pressure on the river. In response to the expected demand on the fishery, a project to evaluate the resource and formulate a management plan was completed between 1975 and 1980. This led to some interesting observations and a change in philosophy by the department. Fish and game has always been reluctant to adopt special regulations for sections of water, particularly so if there wasn't a perceived biological need. It was felt that special regulations were social in effect and excluded portions of the population from the resource. Nevertheless, the study eventually led to special regulations on the upper portion of the river, from the state line to the town of Saratoga. It was found there was a biological need, and this opened the door to a more broad-minded approach to management and an increased willingness to at least examine the possibilities for special regulations on other sections of water.

This study resulted in the cessation of stocking programs in the river upstream of Saratoga in 1979. A wild trout management concept was adopted because it was discovered that the trout could and would be self-sustaining. Evidence of trout reproduction was found in twenty-one of the twenty-six tributary streams sampled. Almost all of the tributaries considered to be spawning habitat flow into the river upstream of Saratoga. Both brown and rainbow trout appear to use the same tributary streams for spawning, although some of the smaller streams, especially those in the Northgate Canyon area, are better used by rainbows. It was also discovered that brown trout likely use the river proper for spawning to a larger and more successful degree than do rainbow trout, due to the heavy springtime water flows and ice scour. Fall dewatering of the smaller streams, especially those diverted for irrigation purposes, is a factor that forces the browns to make more use of the river to spawn.

The wild trout concept study found that at the cessation of the stocking programs there was an approximate eighty-nine percent increase in the trout population, and most dramatically in the rainbow population. This was a huge success, but a problem was soon detected. The size structure of the wild trout population was being altered due to a selective fishing harvest. Fish in catchable sizes were being culled from the general population by fishermen keeping their limits. These were the fish larger than about ten inches and about two years old, which were mostly breedable fish. If something wasn't done, the population of breeders would be severely depleted and the management plan might backfire. It was determined that reducing the number allowed in the creel limit would not protect these fish. It might have slowed down the depletion, but eventually enough of these fish would be eliminated from the population to severely curtail a self-sustaining reproduction program.

This problem prompted fish and game to set some goals to preserve and protect the wild trout fishery. They attempted to reduce the mortality of trout greater than ten inches to an average of forty to fifty percent a year; maintain an approximate population of 2,500 trout per kilometer, of which thirty-five to forty-five percent are greater than ten inches; provide anglers with the opportunity to catch a larger-than-average wild trout; and increase the catch rate by three times. To accomplish these goals, a slot limit was established for the river above Saratoga. The limit allowed anglers to take six trout per day using flies or artificial lures, only one of which could exceed sixteen inches, and all fish in the slot between ten and sixteen inches must be released unharmed.

Since the slot limit has been put into effect, results have indicated a huge success story for this portion of the river. The wild trout fishery has given a positive response, with an increase in the numbers of trout in the target (slot) group and an increase in the overall numbers of trout per mile. Fishermen are releasing more fish outside the slot size; about half of the fish over sixteen inches are being released. The slot has not resulted in an increased harvest of fish less than ten inches. There also appears to be an apparent trend to more of a catch-and-release philosophy on the part of the anglers.

These special regulations have made for better quality fishing on this section of river. The conservation-minded attitude of more anglers has certainly aided the preservation of this section of river and appears to be continuing. The anticipated growth in human population in Wyoming never did materialize, so this section of river is fortunate to have had a protective set of regulations established without a huge increase in fishing pressure. As more and more anglers discover this fishery the pressure will surely increase, but at least these regulations will insure that the quality of this magnificent wild trout fishery will be retained.

Seasonal Changes in Fishing

Weather plays a significant role in the fishability of this portion of river. The high elevation of this Rocky Mountain region keeps the river in the throes of winter for a longer period of time than it does the lower sections. Accessibility to the river is also dependent on the weather, especially so on the east side of the river, where most of the roads travel through the forest. The river may be clear enough to fish but the roads into it might still be snow-covered enough to prevent access. The road along the west side of the river has a better chance of being passable, but an early fall or spring storm could change that rather quickly. It is always a good idea to pay attention to weather forecasts when venturing to this section of river, especially so in the spring, early summer, and fall.

In the early season, air temperature also is a factor in fishing. Once runoff begins and the river is unfishable, a sudden cold snap for a few days could retard the runoff and actually allow the river to clear enough to fish. The tributaries will cease dumping excess water into the river and the flows will slow, causing the water level to drop a few inches. This drop in the river is noticeable as far downstream as Saratoga, where many of the local fishermen keep an eye on water levels. When levels begin to drop in the midst of runoff, it acts as a signal that the river upstream is fishable. Fishermen who live in the area can get some fishing in at a moment's notice by watching water levels. I am always surprised to find that the river has been fishable upstream when it is roiling with runoff in the Rawlins area.

Immediately after runoff, the water is at its peak level for floating. The flows are fast enough to allow a floating fisherman to cover the great distances between access points without spending inordinate amounts of time on the water: twenty to thirty miles a day can be floated in reasonable periods of time. Also, the water is high enough that the fish will hold the banks. The white-water enthusiast will find the upper portion of this section to his liking as some of the rapids become less dangerous and more navigable.

As the season progresses to summer, water levels drop and the float fisherman will begin experiencing difficulties. The rock-strewn river course will require more maneuvering around boulders, and the shallow areas might require some portaging. Float times become dramatically longer, and water that should be fished now has to be floated over. This upper stretch is mostly abandoned by local floating fishermen now, because it is simply too much of a hassle to endure when there is more floatable water downstream.

The wade fisherman will find midsummer and fall to be ideal for his pursuits. Most of the river here is wadable, and water can be adequately covered by walking. The weather is generally pleasant, with warm days and cool nights, and the water is clear. A severe thunderstorm could botch up the fishing, but the water clears quickly in this section. The later one gets into the season, the more the water seems to take on pocket-water character. This is ideal for the wading angler, for he can effectively work sections of the river and be reasonably sure there are fish holding there.

Once the snow starts falling, this section of river begins to shut down. Not so much because the river is unfishable, but because access to it becomes a problem, if not dangerous. Once winter hits, the river snuggles in under a blanket of snow and ice to wait it out until spring.

Spring (March, April, and May)

This is a tough time of year for the angler to find any decent fishing opportunities on this stretch of river. Ice, snow, runoff, and stormy weather all combine to make it difficult to fish. It isn't impossible—there are short times of fishable water—but there are so many variables that accurately predicting when the fishing will be good is a job best left to the fortune-tellers. A year with little stored precipitation and an early warming trend will find the river fishable much earlier than normal. Or, a year with normal precipitation and a very gradual warming might possibly find the river fishable during the normal runoff period as night-time air temperatures retard the flows from the tributaries.

One never knows what to expect from the river here. Fishing could be excellent in April or May some years and the river a raging torrent in others. March is almost always bad. (I don't even look to this section of river until May for any fishing.) Anglers who live in the Saratoga area have a better opportunity to fish this section because it is an easier trip for them to make when they think the river is fishable, based on the flows and water level in town. Any angler finding himself in the Saratoga area during this time should come prepared with fishing gear, just in case. When there is fishable water the nymph fisherman can catch his share of trout using Halfbacks near the bottom because there are all kinds of stonefly nymphs ready to hatch out.

Early Summer (End of May to the Beginning of July)

This could be prime time on this section of river. Chances are that runoff will still be occurring at some time, but as soon as it abates the fishing picks up in full force. A variety of stonefly nymphs literally pave the river bottom but unfortunately hatch out during the runoff. The assortment of stoneflies includes the large *Pteronarcys* species, or giant salmon fly.

One year I gave a slide show for the Federation of Fly Fishers at their annual conclave in Livingston, Montana, and showed slides of the North Platte's upper white-water section. The slides were the typical sort, of rafts being nearly swamped by heavy rapids and guys bailing frantically. I made a comment about how this was a typical early-season fishing trip and went on to talk about the huge numbers of *Pteronarcys* available, thinking I was being humorous. After the slide show, a man told me of his white-water trip there, and how when his party camped for the night he could hear fish slapping the water all night long. Another friend of mine had a similar experience. He was doing the white-water section at a time when the air temperature was dropping. This retarded the runoff and allowed the river to clear. The giant stoneflies had hatched, and the adults were flying about in good numbers. Every time one would land on the water a fish would clobber it. He swears the fishing would have been awesome if he had had his gear with him. No one figures the river to be fishable when these stoneflies hatch out, but there are special conditions that could provide for some super fishing. I think it would be a wise move to always include some fishing gear on any white-water trip to this upper section of the river.

This hatch seems to be confined to the upper reaches of this section of water. I don't know why, but it must have something to do with habitat. It's too bad the hatch takes place during the runoff period and doesn't extend to the lower sections of the river. I have had the good fortune to fish heavy *Pteronarcys* hatches on the Yellowstone River in Montana and cannot think of too many other occasions in fly fishing that compare to it. Having trout savagely smash oversized drys is an event to take part in. Although large stoneflies can be found downstream, they are not in sufficient numbers to cause any wild feeding sprees.

Brown trout tend to be attracted to these large insects to a greater degree than are rainbow trout in the early part of the summer. They seem to select larger food items for which less energy would be expended per calorie ingested. Rainbows tend to feed on a wider range and a larger quantity of food items. The angler fishing for brown trout should keep this in mind. Maybe rainbows have other things on their minds in the early season. It has been discovered that spawning times for rainbow trout can be quite variable in this upper section, many apparently spawn as late as mid-June.

Once the water flows begin to drop and the white-water season is about over, the float fishermen can have excellent fishing. I look for the water to clear so that there is at least eighteen inches of visibility before I begin floating. When this happens the water levels are still relatively high and the water speed is still relatively fast. The water level and speed make it ideal to float the long distances between decent access points. And the flows push the fish to the calmer, slower water along the banks, out of the brunt of the main current. Here they do not have to work so hard just to maintain their position as they lie in wait of food items drifting by. This is the time to throw big stuff to the banks, streamers and large attractor-style nymphs.

Some relatively specialized tackle requirements are necessary, as are some special fishing techniques. This is the time when fishermen using spinning gear usually do exceptionally well. Their success has led me to attempt to analyze the reasons for their effectiveness: mainly, their offerings quickly get to the bottom and stay near it during the retrieve. This is relatively hard to do with fly-fishing tackle because the diameter of the fly line catches the current and tends to pull the fly to the surface, away from where the trout hold. Simply using heavily weighted flies isn't the ticket. It would be if a fisherman just fished the small pockets along the bank, but a good deal of fish taken in this section are hooked as the fly is pulled from the bank into the current toward the boat. As soon as the current catches the fly line, weighted flies are pulled to the surface out of the effective zone.

The spin fisherman can keep his lure near the bottom for a good deal of the retrieve; the thin monofilament line does not create the drag that a thick fly line does. Full-sinking lines, even the very fast ones, are not the ticket either because the densest part of the line is usually the thickest, and that is near the middle of the line. This seems as though it would work well because the thicker part of the line would tend to pull the thinner tip down to it during the retrieve. It does do that and would work fine if one didn't have to take the speed of the current near the boat into account. This current is significantly faster than the current near the bank, and once the line is caught in it, it rapidly pulls the imitation away from the bank—not exactly what one hopes for. Besides, picking a full-sinking line out of the water to make a new cast is an abomination. When floating, it's to one's advantage to be able to quickly pick the line off the water to cast to new water because it does go by rather quickly.

A workable rig is one that gets the imitation down fast and allows it to stay there. I find a sinking-tip fly line very well suited to the task, because the floating section can be manipulated by mending up or downstream to control the amount of drag on the line. Obviously, the less drag there is on the main body of the line, the less likely it is that the drift of the imitation will be affected. A high-density very-fast-sinking tip is my preference, and it should be at least a 7-weight.

One early summer, a few friends and I floated this upper stretch. I was using a 7-weight, one of the guys an 8-weight, and another a 6-weight. Jerry, the friend with the 6-weight, was having some difficulty catching fish; even though he did exactly what we did, his catch rate was low. His 6-weight line, although it was the same brand and style we were using, did not have the sinking power to put his flies in front of fish on the bottom. As soon as he switched to one of our rods he began catching fish at the same rate we did.

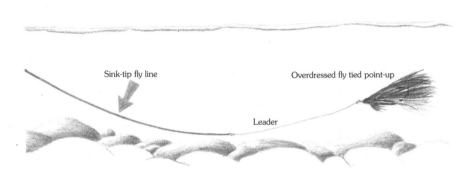

Tackle requirements should include a 7-weight fast-sinking sinking-tip fly line, a short leader, and a rod capable of handling everything. The flies can be weighted or unweighted, this I think depends on the leader design. A relatively short monofilament leader of about three to four feet will require a heavily weighted fly, otherwise it will tend to ride up toward the surface no matter what kind of fly line is used. A short weighted leader, such as a braided leader with lead core, will not require that the fly be weighted because it will act as an extension of the sinking tip and keep the fly down where it belongs.

I am experimenting with using unweighted flies that are slightly over-dressed and tied with the hook in the up position (see the illustration, above). I believe that the overdressing will keep the fly from being driven into the bottom, and the hook-up position of the fly will be less likely to snag on the bottom. So far so good with this experiment. I am even tying mono weedguards on my streamers to keep them from snagging.

Another tackle setup is to use a shooting taper and a floating running line. A good thing about using shooting tapers is that an angler can customize them to suit his needs or different water speeds. By purchasing several, a fisherman can cut them to different lengths so they sink at different rates. Then, by making loop-to-loop connections in the ends and in the end of the running line, he can quickly change heads to meet most floating situations without having to change reel spools. An assortment of heads can fit easily into a vest and be quickly changed. This is a great system for traveling and fishing waters that may be unfamiliar.

A key element in using this setup is to cast as close to the bank as humanly possible, often a mere inch or so from the shore. Anything else is simply not as effective. This is difficult for the average wading fisherman, but the float fisherman has to make his cast as quickly as possible because there is very little time to false-cast and measure distances. Here is where a good guide earns his keep: if he maintains a constant distance between the boat and bank, accurate casting to the shore should be relatively easy. Once the right amount of line is measured, subsequent casts should be about the same. The guide who gets lazy and allows the boat to move into and away from the bank will be the cause for some frustration in missed opportunities or snagged flies. If you are dropping casts where they belong and appear to be casting with the deftness of Lefty Kreh, tip the guide well or at least buy him a beer.

Even if the guide does his job, flies will become snagged in the over-hanging brush or on the bottom—it's in the nature of fishing like this. A fairly stout tippet will allow the angler to pull his fly free of the bottom or from a snag some of the time. I once guided a client who would keep one eye on his presentation and another on the water ahead. If he saw water coming up that looked good to him, he would make a reckless cast to it so he would not miss out on the opportunity. His reck-less casting cost him four dozen lost streamers that day. His comment to me was that he was glad he tied his own flies because he wouldn't have been able to afford the trip otherwise.

When a fly is snagged in the brush, a great deal of care should be taken in trying to pull it free. Stout leaders and springy brush make for an interesting combination when the fly finally does come free. Usually it returns to the boat in the fashion of a bullet, often with the same effect. Many fishermen have worn flies on different parts of their anatomies during float trips, many others have made trips to emergency rooms to have them removed. (A client once stuck a fly into my arm just above my elbow in that loose, tough skin. I could not reach it to remove it and he was too squeamish, so I had to wait until the trip was over to have an emergency-room doctor remove it. Every time I made a stroke on the oars it felt like a bee stinging my arm. I was real glad to get off the water that day.)

I usually use barbless hooks or at least bend the barbs down. On one trip I reached over to bend down the barb on one of my client's flies. He discussed the merits of bent barbs in releasing fish while he made his next cast, which promptly became snagged in an overhanging tree. He was asking me if easier releasing was the reason for bending down barbs when his fly pulled free of the tree and came zipping back to the boat to embed itself in the meaty part of the ball of my thumb. "No, this is why," I said as I slid the hook out of my hand and handed it back to him. "Oh," was his only reply.

Streamers are the ticket at this time, and the Woolly Bugger is king. Black and olive are generally all one needs, but there are occasions when other colors are more effective. The Yellow and Black Bugger has absolutely hammered fish on many trips when all else failed. This is a super-effective pattern on this section of river. A pure white Woolly Bugger has been effective for me during bright cloudless days. Large attractor-style nymphs like Bitch Creeks, Girdle Bugs, Yuk Bugs, and large Half-backs are also relatively effective at this time. "The bigger the better" is the adage to follow when the water is high and dirty.

Once the water begins to drop, floating becomes more and more impractical because of the difficulty of maneuvering around the rocks and the shallowness of the water. Most people look to lower sections of river to float. But the fishing remains good here, and the wading angler can get his licks in. There is plenty of surface activity at this time, and the nymph fisherman will always take some fish. I consider the caddis to be the most important insect on this section at this time of year. The long shallow riffles make for ideal caddis water and are classic wet-fly and soft-hackle situations. Swinging one of these patterns down and across the current is an easy and effective technique and does catch its share of fish.

The nymph fisherman will find that most caddis larva or emerger patterns will be effective to some degree. The Bead Head Caddis larva is the new "hot" pattern on this stretch of river. The Halfback in a #8 is one of the most productive patterns for this upper reach. Smaller mayfly nymph patterns will also do the job because most of the mayflies are about ripe and ready to hatch at this time. Speaking of mayflies, one should be on the lookout for the little blue-winged olive (*Baetis*). Pods of fish rising to these insects can be found on some of the slower glides along the banks. There is also a variety of variously sized stoneflies that hatch sporadically during this early-summer period. Work some

Where the Encampment River flows into the North Platte, there are usually rising fish.

of the faster water with a Golden Stone dry or large attractor-style dry flies for some interesting action.

The mouth of the Encampment River as it dumps into the North Platte always seems to have rising fish in it and along the current edge where it meets the river. The Encampment clears earlier than the North Platte does, so there is always a tongue of clear water to fish. One can hardly refuse an opportunity to cast to these fish, even though the banks are on private property. Floating by only allows for a few casts before the current takes the boat downstream. It is real difficult not to anchor on the tiny island here and get out of the boat to fish to these rising trout. I suspect most anglers do just that—there have been times when these fish were the only ones I caught all day.

Midsummer (July and August)

This is the time for classic fly fishing, or at least what I grew up thinking was classic fly fishing: low water and fish feeding on the surface. The midsummer months find this section of river with low flows that are wadable and, comparatively, much easier to deal with. The floating season is effectively over, although one will see canoes, kayaks, and rafts drifting down the river, but the folks with drift boats have migrated to the lower stretches of water. This is the time for light watercraft and some camping gear. The lower flows extend the time needed to float, so the best way to deal with it is to take some time and camp along the way. The upper reach in the national forest area is ideal for this type of trip because there are plenty of campsites along the way.

The Northgate Canyon area at this time is the ultimate spot for the backpacking fisherman. The steep canyon environment protects it from the casual day-tripper, especially the farther one gets from the access area. The water is low and takes on the character of a pocket-water fishery but on a large scale, and the best element of this formula is that there is virtually no fishing pressure. The weather is generally decent— warm days and cool nights—and the scenery is magnificent.

The Sixmile Gap area is another spot that lends itself to a backpack-fishing trip. Pickaroon, the next access site downstream, is only about eight and a half miles away. This distance can easily be covered in a couple of days and still allow quality fishing. Conditions similar to the canyon above exist, but there is slightly more pressure. A popular summer float in a raft or canoe is from Sixmile Gap to Pickaroon or even as far down as Bennett Peak. These trips more than likely will require a night or two at campsites, especially the Bennett Peak float, which is about twenty-six miles. The low flows make for slow going but offer the angler the opportunity to take his time and fully enjoy the trip. The angler can stop, get out of the boat, and fish the good-looking water in the national forest area or on public land.

The angler who prefers to drive can do so at the Pickaroon and Bennett Peak sites. Here he can fish for the day or spend as much time as he wants camping and fishing.

Plenty happens on the water in midsummer; there is a wide assortment of insects for the trout to feed on. There are some decent mayfly hatches, caddis are still going strong, and there are sporadic hatches of stoneflies to keep the fisherman occupied. The pale morning dun makes its appearance in fair numbers. The duns hatch out in the late morning and last for a couple of hours, providing some classic dry-fly fishing. They generally hatch out of the riffles, and some fish can be seen feeding in the riffles or in the current edges alongside the riffles. The majority of fish will feed in the downstream slower sections of water, where they do not have to expend more energy than necessary to feed. Any current edge of moderate to slow speed that funnels or concentrates these insects will have trout sipping them from the surface. The rise-forms are on the subtle side and often easy to miss, especially if the hatch is not heavy. The bright, clear days bring lighter hatches than do the overcast, dull days. The hatches on this upper section of river are usually not as thick as farther on downstream, but they do occur here in sufficient numbers to entice pods of fish to feed on the surface.

Even though the hatch doesn't get going full-tilt until late morning, the fish are usually on the nymphs. Any stocky-bodied, tannish mayfly nymph imitation in #16 will take fish during this period. Of course, the more specific imitations are effective but not necessary because the trout in this area are not very pressured. As long as the presentation is decent, the fish will rarely refuse the offering. Fish these nymphs dead-drift along the bottom and expect strikes anywhere in the drift. At the end of the drift, allow the nymph to swing with the current. This will imitate an emerging nymph rising to the surface and can be extremely effective immediately before the duns are on the surface. When large numbers of duns begin to hatch, there is a transitional period when some of the fish key on the emergers. This can be tough because some fish will be on duns, some on emergers, and others will still be feeding on the nymphs. Careful observation can help an angler distinguish when a particular fish is feeding on a dun or emerger and perhaps cover the bases and fish two flies.

Tie on an emerger pattern as a point fly and a dun pattern as a dropper: this could help take some of the guesswork out of the presentation. Eventually, most of the fish will switch to the duns until the hatch peters out. The spinners return to the water in the late afternoon and evening. I have never witnessed a major spinner fall here, but I have taken fish with a spentwing pattern in the evening. A rusty spinner imitation fished in the slower sections of water wherever currents concentrate the naturals should produce a few fish. The tailouts of pools are other areas where spentwing patterns are effective—the trout seem to hold right above the riffles in the smooth water.

Caddisflies can hatch at about the same time in the early part of this period, and then much later in the afternoon as the season progresses. A pattern that I like to fish when there are both PMDs and caddis on the water is kind of a combination of the two. It has the tails, body, and hackle of a PMD dun and the wing and head are tied in the style of an Elk Hair Caddis, but instead of elk hair I use the gray portion of deer hair. I think some fish take it for a caddis and others for the PMD.

Fishing the actual caddis hatch is exciting and relatively simple; presentations are hard to screw up because even a dragging artificial can resemble the actions of a caddis skating or running across the surface. The evening flights of caddis are also exciting to fish, because the caddis return to the water to lay eggs. Some dap the surface with their abdomens and others actually dive into the water and swim to the bottom to lay their eggs. All this activity does get the trout's attention. I find that a diving caddis pattern fished with a wet-fly swing through the riffles works well.

This is an extremely easy way to fish and is especially suited to the novice fly fisherman. Long, delicate, and accurate casts are not necessary. All that needs to be done is to get the pattern out in the current either directly across from the angler or quartering downstream. Once the fly is in the current, the angler should do nothing but let it swing until it is hanging directly downstream from him, then give it a couple of twitches and recast. The riffle should be covered from top to bottom and from near to far. Sometimes actually hooking a fish will be a little tricky because the striking motion on the angler's part will pull the fly back upstream and away from the fish, but mostly the fish hook themselves during the take.

An effective local fly is the Platte River Carey. It more than likely imitates a caddis pupa or a mayfly emerger, but it isn't fished as one. This is an all-purpose pattern that has many uses: it can be presented to rising fish, fished wet, or fished blind. A few local guides have relied on this pattern to help clients new to the sport of fly fishing. When fish were rising, and relatively accurate casts or presentations were necessary, they would have their clients swing a Platte River Carey in front of the fish, often with good results. It is easier to allow a fly to swing in front of a fish than it is to present a dry fly in a feeding lane with a drag-free drift. A Carey fished through a riffle on a classic wet-fly swing has saved many a day for me. There have been a few days when nothing seemed to be happening on the surface and the fish just didn't appear to be in the feeding mode. A Carey worked through a riffle was just the ticket, turning a fishless day into one filled with excitement. Another method is to fish it to the banks and any likely water from a boat. This is blind fishing in the sense that the angler isn't casting to any visible fish and generally cannot see his imitation.

Tricorythodes species, or Tricos, are a major part of surface activity at this time. As one walks along the river in the Sixmile Gap area during the morning hours, huge mating swarms of these tiny insects will be seen, appearing like columns of smoke. One rarely fishes the actual hatch because the males hatch out overnight and the females hatch in the wee dawn hours. The spinner fall is the event in this insect's life cycle to fish. In the morning hours after they hatch, the Tricos swarm to mate and immediately begin the egg-laying process. The female duns die and fall to the water after ejecting their eggs, and the males follow a little later. In some areas, these spent Tricos are so numerous that they literally blanket the water's surface. Trout do key on these minute mayflies and, because of their abundance, become selective to them. The trout will move to the slower water along shore, often only a few inches deep, to leisurely sip in the spentwings. This generally takes place around nine o'clock in the morning and lasts until around eleven.

Presentation is the key to catching fish when the Trico spinners are on the water. This is not to say that pattern isn't important—it is. The imitation should be in the general ballpark regarding size and color. A dark-bodied fly in #18 to #20 will almost always take fish if presented correctly. Once the trout establish themselves in feeding lanes, they will not move very far to take an artificial. Their feeding lanes bring all the food they could want right to their noses. The presentation should be made right in the feeding lane so a fish does not have to think about moving. The presentation should also be drag-free. The Trico spinners are dead and certainly unable to move—any drag will cause a refusal.

Trout feeding on Trico spinners will usually be found in the slower or shallower water. The larger fish take over the easier and richer feeding stations and force the smaller fish to the less-than-ideal areas. It is a good bet that the largest fish will be closest to the banks in the prime water. Careful approaches are suggested so that fish are not put down.

There is a wide assortment of other species of mayfly that hatch in small numbers, certainly not great enough to cause wild feeding sprees on the part of the trout. This enables the fly fisherman to use an assortment of dry-fly patterns to prospect for fish when there are very few fish rising. An occasional fish will rise and take an insect off the surface when there isn't an apparent hatch, sometimes it will do so continually. This fish may be opportunistically feeding on whatever happens to be drifting by, or it may be on a very minor and localized hatch. It really should not be too difficult to take a fish like this, especially if the presentation is right on the money, because the fishing pressure is so light it probably has not yet learned to be pattern-selective. One of the minor mayfly hatches is the pale evening dun, which emerges in the late afternoon and evening. A #14 or #16 Light Cahill, Gray Fox, or Ginger Quill will do an adequate job of imitating it.

The summer months will find a variety of stoneflies available to the trout. There are always stonefly nymphs on the bottom for trout to feed on. This is important for the nymph fisherman to know, so that he may imitate them. The large *Pteronarcys* species have mostly hatched out, but an occasional one will still be seen fluttering about. There are some little yellow stoneflies available. These are about the size and general shape of the abundant caddis, and the golden stone and brown willow flies hatch sporadically. The good news is that an angler can fish relatively large attractor-style dry flies, such as a Stimulator, and reasonably expect to catch fish. These stoneflies get blown or fall to the water's surface, where trout will opportunistically feed on them.

In the forested areas of this section it is always a good idea to have a few ant patterns in red and black. These terrestrials do end up in the water and become food items for the fish. Sometimes a fair amount of ants end up in the water and create a minihatch, much to the confusion of many anglers. Besides, ant patterns always seem to take a few fish no matter where they may be used.

The midsummer months offer the fly fisherman a wide variety of things to do both on and off the water. The insects available are varied enough to suit the needs of most people, as are the fishing techniques used. It is the time of plenty and of plenty of fun.

The river near Bennett Peak in the autumn.

Fall (September, October, and November)

As the days begin to shorten and the nights get cooler and crisper, the hatches of the summer months wane. The early fall will still find some Tricos but they will soon diminish and the little *Baetis* species will begin to appear. Caddis will be available but become more and more sporadic as the season progresses. It becomes a matter of being in the right riffle at the right time to hit a decent caddis emergence. The *Baetis* will begin the season by hatching around eleven o'clock in the morning but will hatch progressively later in the day as the season moves on. These insects will hatch until the weather simply gets too cold—sometimes this happens in October.

An interesting aspect of trout behavior is that little fish are more generalized in their feeding habits and larger fish become more selective. This is very apparent during the fall months in this section of water. Brown trout seem to selectively seek out the variety of large stonefly nymphs to make up a major portion of their diet, and the rainbows are keyed to the mayfly hatches still occurring. This is important to the fisherman, because if he is after a decent-sized brown trout he knows he probably should be using stonefly imitations fished along the bottom. An angler will take both species if he is fishing a *Baetis* hatch, but the majority of brown trout in his catch will be small. The fish between ten and fourteen inches aren't as picky about what they eat.

Later in the fall, the brown trout will begin their spawning rituals. By this time of year most fishermen have given up fishing this area, so the fish are left to themselves. The late fall is probably the time of year, with the exception of winter, that sees the least amount of fishing pressure on this upper stretch. The fishing remains excellent but, for whatever reasons, most fishermen are fishing other areas or doing something else. I suppose this is a good thing, leaving the spawning browns alone to reproduce and flourish.

Winter comes early to this high-altitude section of river, effectively shutting down any fishing opportunities. Ice and snow blanket the river, and the trout are left to survive this winter wonderland.

Locally Effective Patterns

Halfback

Hook:	4-12
Thread:	Black
Tail:	Pheasant-tail fibers
Abdomen:	Peacock herl
Shellback:	Thick bunch of pheasant-tail fibers pulled over the abdomen
Thorax:	Peacock herl
Hackle:	Brown, palmered over thorax

Yellow and Black Bugger

Hook:	2-8
Thread:	Black
Tail:	Black over yellow marabou with a few strands of pearl Flashabou
Body:	Yellow chenille
Shellback:	Black marabou pulled over body
Hackle:	Black, palmered over body

PMD/Caddis

Hook:	12-18
Thread:	Gray
Tails:	Medium blue dun Micro Fibetts, split and divided
Body:	Light sulphur or yellowish green dubbing
Wing:	Deer hair, caddis style
Hackle:	Medium blue dun
Head:	Clipped deer hair, tied Elk Hair Caddis style

Platte River Carey

Hook:	10-18
Thread:	Black
Tail:	Four to six peacock swords, the bluer the better
Body:	Peacock herl
Hackle:	Pheasant rump feather, the bluer the better

Bead Head Caddis Larva

Hook:	10-16
Thread:	Black
Ribbing:	Copper wire
Abdomen:	Light hare's ear dubbing
Thorax:	Dark hare's ear dubbing
Head:	Brass bead

Other Effective Patterns

Adams
PMD Dun
Comparadun
Pale Evening Dun
Light Cahill
Gray Fox
Ginger Quill
Blue Dun
Little Blue-Winged Olive
Royal Wulff

Humpy
Red or black ants
Elk Hair Caddis
Bucktail caddis
Stimulator
Yellow Sally
Sofa Pillow
Bird's Stonefly
Golden Stone
Gold-Ribbed Hare's Ear

Pheasant Tail
Caddis larva
Box Canyon Stone
Yellow Stone Nymph
Diving caddis
Emergent caddis
Woolly Buggers (black, olive, white)
Platte River Special
Cranefly larva

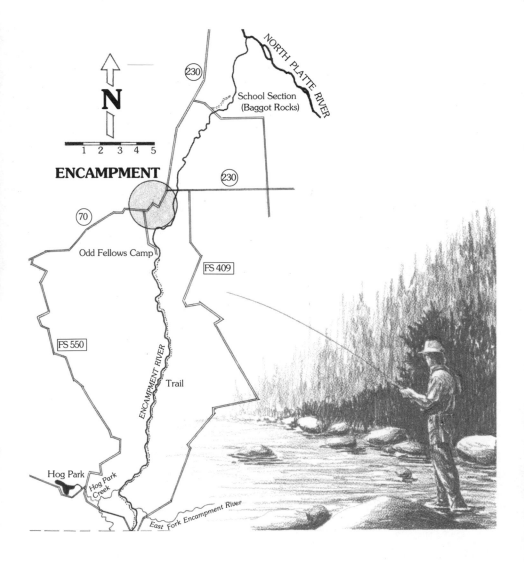

N

1 2 3 4 5

(230)

NORTH PLATTE RIVER

School Section
(Baggot Rocks)

ENCAMPMENT

(230)

(70)

Odd Fellows Camp

FS 409

FS 550

ENCAMPMENT RIVER

Trail

Hog Park

Hog Park Creek

East Fork Encampment River

4

The Encampment River

The first time I ever stepped in the Encampment River a blizzard of a caddis hatch was occurring and fish were wildly rising everywhere I looked. I wasn't prepared for what I saw and spent an inordinate amount of time fumbling with my equipment. The anticipation of actually fishing this hatch sent adrenalin surges through my body, making it almost impossible to tie a knot. Eventually I got my act together to catch the first fish, the one that takes all the pressure off an angler and allows him to actually enjoy the rest of the day. I spent the next hour or so frenetically attempting to catch every fish in the river and could do no wrong. The excitement of the moment added to the inaccuracy of my casts—my presentations were terrible and my fly dragged more often than it drifted, but it didn't matter. I caught fish after fish, as fast as I could.

The hatch eventually tapered off and my pulse rate slowed to near normal as the afternoon wore on. The rest of the day was anticlimatic, with a fish here and a fish there, but who cared. As I returned to my truck and stowed my gear, I realized that I had taken part in a very special event. A hatch of that intensity doesn't occur very often, and I was more than a little surprised to witness it. As it turned out, that wasn't the last time this little river surprised me.

The Encampment River already is part of the history of fly fishing. Ray Bergman wrote about fishing the Encampment with streamers in *Trout*. It was once a utilitarian river in the time of the copper mines, and to this day there are sections near town that will not hold fish because of pollution from the mine tailings. But, thank goodness, most of the river is pure and pristine, with the ability to hold a great deal of fish.

Topography

The headwaters of this little river are in Colorado and enter Wyoming in the mountains of the Medicine Bow National Forest, where smaller tributaries join to form the main river. It then runs down a fairly steep gradient for the next sixteen miles through a canyonlike area into the small town of Encampment. This town is rich in mining lore and has a small museum that should be visited. From the town to its confluence with the North Platte River, the Encampment flows through ranch bottomland. The terrain changes from a rugged mountain environment to the flatter, gentler contours of hay fields. The change is gradual as the river flows through transitional foothill terrain that is mostly open, sage-covered land.

Water Characteristics

The river runs the full gamut of water types on its journey to the North Platte. The upstream sections can be white-water torrents when the flows are high because the riverbed gradient is quite steep. When the water levels drop, the river turns into a pocket-water fishery. Huge boulders are strewn throughout this section, both in the water and along its banks, creating deep holes as the water rushes around them. The cascading rapidlike areas are interspersed with deep pools and smaller pockets of deep water, all of which will hold fish. This is the general character of the water in the upper sixteen miles as it flows down from the mountains.

The remainder of the river flows through a far less steep gradient as it winds its way through various ranches. Here the river's character changes to a slower, deeper, and more meandering one. It still is a pocket-water fishery because of its size, but the lower stretch has more of the character of a larger river. There are riffles, runs, pools, and glides. There are undercut banks, deep holes, and sharp changes of direction forming those great inside bends for the nymph fisherman. Vegetation overhangs or has fallen into the water, creating holding areas. There are some areas of braiding, especially when the flows are low, where the river flows around tiny islands. The lower section will even find a small reservoir formed by a dam some six or eight feet high. This dam is the only thing that prevents anglers from floating in canoes or small rafts or boats down the lower sections of the river to the North Platte. Portages are nearly impossible around the dam, and access is through private property.

There are some surprisingly deep sections in this little river. A friend of mine, who is rather on the short side, and I were walking along the river's edge during a fishing trip. We were both in the water searching for rising fish. I wasn't paying attention to where I was walking and down I went into a deep hole created by a small backwater. I was chest-deep and staring at his kneecaps as the water began to fill my waders. He turned, looked down, and began to laugh uncontrollably. The twists and turns of the currents carve out some very deep spots in the river at some very innocent-looking places. Generally, an angler can get by with hip boots, but waders are more appropriate for fishing the deeper sections. There are sections where an angler needs to fish from the water because of the overhanging vegetation, and the freedom to cross the stream at any point is an advantage.

Accessibility

About half of the river is accessible to the fly fisherman, even though there are only three access points. The first access point is a state school section at Baggot Rocks. A mile of river is accessible on this lower stretch. One would think this access point would be crowded because of its proximity to Saratoga and Encampment, but every time I have fished here I have had it pretty much to myself. The water in this area is typical bottomland water, with more gentle flows than in the upstream sections.

The second access point is at the Oddfellows camp just south of Encampment. Overnight camping is allowed here. The angler can fish in the general area or he can walk up the trail on the east side of the river as far as he feels comfortable fishing back. This is the beginning of approximately sixteen miles of accessible river because the hiking trail makes its way to Hog Park Reservoir. I had wanted to take my mountain bike on this trail to ride, fish, and camp, but no mechanical devices are allowed on this national forest trail. This is a good access for the fisherman who wants to walk a distance and fish his way back to vehicle or camp, because he can work his way back downhill. The water type at this access is general pocket water, more so the farther upstream one goes.

The third access point is at the Hog Park Reservoir area, where there is plenty of room to camp. There is a campground with primitive restroom facilities and, of course, one can camp practically anywhere in the national forest. An angler can stay here and have all kinds of fishing opportunities. Hog Park Creek is a tiny tailwater fishery that flows from the dam into the Encampment River, where it meets the trail. One can fish down Hog Park Creek and then hit the upper Encampment River, fishing either upstream or down. A popular trip is to arrange a shuttle from Hog Park to the Oddfellows camp and backpack down the sixteen-mile trail, fishing and camping along the way. It is a downhill walk that could easily be done in a weekend, but three days would be ideal, giving one plenty of time to stop and fish the likely looking spots.

The roads into the access sites are more than adequate, and even though some are gravel, they are in good condition. The river is within easy driving distance from Saratoga, so anyone in the area fishing the North Platte can make a quick side trip to fish some different water for a few hours.

Management Practices

Brown trout and rainbows reside in the lower sections of the river. As one moves farther upstream, brook trout begin to make an appearance. The size of the average fish changes with the character of the river: the slower, lower sections will hold larger fish than will the mountainous upper portions. Every piece of water has tales of monster fish residing in its depths, and the Encampment is no exception. A friend tells me of an eight-pound brown yanked from one of the deeper holes by a bait fisherman. I don't doubt it because I know the nature of the water in the lower section of the river. It is easy to believe a fish could attain a mammoth size in the cover of the depths while preying on smaller trout. Generally, most of the fish caught here will be much smaller, with an occasional fish approaching twenty inches.

Currently, the river is managed as a basic yield fishery (fish are stocked) supported by wild trout. There are plans for some changes in the management of the fishery that include a change to a total wild trout concept. Improvements to habitat at the Baggot Rocks School section and the Oddfellows camp are also on tap, along with the encouragement of habitat improvements on private lands. There are plans to purchase approximately two miles of additional easements that will improve access to otherwise private land.

Other goals for the river include a 15-cfs minimum flow. A goal of utmost importance to the fisherman is for the fish and game department to attain a population of approximately 2,500 wild trout per mile, with at least 115 of these fish greater than fourteen inches. Monitoring will take place at the Baggot Rocks School section. Public meetings are slated for the future to discuss these goals and any others. This is in keeping with fish and game's willingness to listen to what the public wants in the way of fisheries. I imagine that if enough of a fuss were raised by the public to make the Encampment River a trophy fishery, then fish and game would take a long hard look at it, provided it was biologically feasible to do so.

Although the Encampment River is an important tributary to the North Platte River, the movement of fish into it from the North Platte is severely impaired. In 1986 a fish ladder was installed at the irrigation diversion on the Encampment to allow fish passage to and from the river. It immediately failed due to structural design, thereby preventing fish from entering the river. If a successful fish ladder can be constructed, then there may be a significant benefit to the Encampment and the North Platte. Spawning trout, especially brown trout in the fall, would be able to use this important tributary. Money seems to be the fly in the ointment preventing a new ladder from being installed. Here is a case where public outcry can possibly speed up the process, but so far the public has been relatively silent.

Seasonal Changes in Fishing

This little river undergoes some abrupt changes over the course of a year. The frozen winter waters give way to the rushing torrents of snowmelt during the spring runoff. The high water gradually recedes to the normal flows of summer, and these gradually give way to the low water of late summer and fall. Weather plays an important role in the level and clarity of the water. Heavy summer rains will wash debris and sediment into the river, discoloring it beyond any reasonable fish-ability. Droughtlike conditions will drop the water levels, creating a pooling effect on the river.

Generally, the Encampment clears earlier in the spring than does the North Platte. It is always a surprise to find it fishable when the North Platte is still high and discolored. When summer thunderstorms muck up the rivers, this one will almost always clear faster than will the big river. Keep this in mind when a summer squall ruins the fishing on the North Platte. At least check out the Encampment—it might be fishable.

Spring (March, April, and May)

The river may be fishable prior to the runoff period during the March thaw. Warm early-spring temperatures at the lower elevations can bring a brief period when the river is ice-free and clear; usually the river will also be low. At this time, cold temperatures will still dominate the higher elevations, retarding the melting snow that brings about the runoff. In years with low levels of precipitation, the river will assuredly be fishable at this time. Of course, we are limited to the lower sections of the river, because the upper reaches can still be locked in the clutches of Old Man Winter. Besides, the trail will surely still be snowed in.

This is the time when attractor-type nymphs much like a Halfback will catch a few decent fish. It is the time of year when rainbows begin their spawning routines. Some large fish (eighteen to twenty inches) are in abundance throughout the lower river. These fish most likely spend a good deal of time in the small reservoir at the lower end of the river during the winter months because of the deeper water there. They move up into the river searching for spawning grounds and remain until water levels drop or get too warm during the summer months. The short prerunoff period may or may not coincide with the actual spawning of these fish; however, it does find these fish in ample supply. If redds are present and fish are obviously on them, then the ethical thing to do is leave them to complete their reproductive activities. At times, fish on redds can be ridiculously easy to catch, but who knows what kind of stress is placed on them by the harassment of angling. Take no chances and pass on these fish; there will be plenty of other fish to take up the slack.

This short period may find some midge activity in the slower sections of the lower river. Fish will very often feed in small pods on these tiny insects, presenting the opportunity to fish with dry flies to the fisherman. A Griffith's Gnat is a good general pattern at this time. Dry-fly fishing can be extremely spotty during this period, so the best bet for the fisherman is to fish subsurface. Caddis larva are abundant and approaching maturity; mayfly nymphs are also reaching a size that interests the fish, and there are stonefly nymphs available. General nymph patterns take fish, and a #14 to #16 Gold-Ribbed Hare's Ear will work well enough. This is a good time to use small Woolly Buggers to imitate the little baitfish that are in ample supply.

As spring hits the Encampment in full force, the fishable water diminishes. Runoff starts, and the river becomes a torrent of high dirty water. This is the time to fish the local reservoirs and ponds. They offer some excellent fishing while the rivers run dirty.

Sometime during the month of May, the river once again becomes fishable. It may be high and the flows semi-fast, but it will be much clearer than the North Platte. This is the time to use nymph patterns, because many mayflies are nearing their periods of emergence. There may be some caddis activity in some of the riffles, providing a good chance to use dry flies. Small streamer patterns are also fairly productive, especially if the fisherman can work the river edges along the banks. It's like floating a river and throwing streamers into pockets and cover along the banks, except in this case the fisherman is walking and wading. An angler can easily cast across this small river to work the opposite bank. Weighted patterns or a sinking-tip line will help sink the imitation quickly, before the currents play havoc with the presentation.

Most of the fishable water is again confined to the lower portion of the river. The upper section is flowing too fast down the steep gradient, and the water will be too high to fish. Fast, high water presents too many problems for productive fishing.

Summer (June, July, and August)

Some amazing things happen in the summer on the Encampment River. There are larger fish in the river in the early part of the summer than one might think given the size of the water. On a good day, a fisherman can catch many rainbows in the seventeen-to-twenty-inch range on the lower section of river. I have had many a day when almost

The lower Encampment River

all the fish I caught fell into that size slot. These fish were all healthy acrobatic fish that put on quite a show in the smaller water.

One early summer I had access to some private water on the lower section of the river when the water was still high but clear. Nymph fishing was excellent, but the most fun was during the almost daily caddis hatches. An occasional small fish would be taken, but the majority were those seventeen- to twenty-inch rainbows that are a ball to catch—flashy leaps followed by long, strong runs. The caddis hatched out late in the morning and provided a few hours of super fishing.

There are some sporadic hatches of smaller mayflies, including the little blue-winged olive. Fish will often be spotted feeding on these mayflies, but the hatches aren't major. There is a little of this and a little of that happening, just enough that the dry-fly enthusiast can use general patterns, like an Adams, to take fish.

I used to think the Encampment River was primarily a caddis river with only a smattering of mayflies. This all changed one early June when a client of mine called to say that he just obtained a lease on some private

water. He said he would like me to accompany him and his wife so
that I could show them how to fish the river. After I received his call,
I sat down at the vise and began tying caddis patterns. I tied all kinds
of imitations—larva, deep pupa, emergent pupa, and various adult
patterns—so I could blind them with my fly-fishing brilliance. I would
have all the bases covered when it came to fishing caddis: I had a plan.
I would kick-screen the water, identify the different stages of a caddis's
development, and then whip out the appropriate pattern to match each
stage. It would be awesome.

I met the client and his wife at their cabin and, as was our custom,
went to have breakfast. Over coffee we talked fishing—what was to be
expected, how we would fish, and what patterns we would use. I
explained that there usually was caddis activity at this time of year. Once
we arrived at the river and geared up, things began to fall apart. I kick-
screened a riffle, fully expecting to see all kinds of caddis in various stages
of development but was totally stunned when I looked at the screen.
"Er, ah, mmm," was all I managed to say as I examined the hundreds
of large mayfly nymphs that totally covered the screen. "Let's kick
another spot," I mumbled, absolutely confused by the turn of events.
We did, and the same thing happened. They looked to me to explain
what was covering the kick-screen, and I was about to admit defeat when
it dawned on me what these nymphs were. "Holy cow!" I screamed.
"These are green drake nymphs!"

The riffle was covered with the nymphs, and I was totally unpre-
pared. I searched through my fly boxes, looking past all those great
caddis imitations to find something resembling a green drake. Finally
I spotted a few #8 Halfbacks and figured they were as close as I could
come. I boldly announced that these were the imitations we would use
and tied them on. Soon after, both my friends were into fish, and a
wave of relief washed over me. Now all I had to worry about was that
they wouldn't lose the flies because I only had a couple left. The fishing
gods were with us: they caught a fair number of decent fish in that
seventeen-to-twenty-inch class, didn't lose the flies, and I still looked
like I knew what I was doing.

I was excited by what I had learned and kept returning to the river
to discover just when the nymphs would hatch out. No one that I had
ever talked to about the Encampment had any idea there were green

drakes in the river. About the third week in June the drakes started to hatch, and I experienced super fishing without any competition. No one knew—I had the hatch all to myself. It was extremely difficult to keep quiet about it, so I only told a few people, most of whom thought I was out of my mind. For a few years one friend and I would meet at the Encampment to fish this hatch in blissful isolation. But all good things come to an end: other fishermen discovered the hatch, and it is now relatively common knowledge.

Prior to the actual hatch, a fisherman can have good fishing with a green drake nymph imitation for a few weeks. The hatch takes place in the late morning to early afternoon. Fishing with huge dun patterns on this tiny stream seems ridiculous, but it is effective and the fish do key on them. Later in the evenings a green drake spinner pattern is effective. The hatch lasts for two to three weeks before it tapers off. Obviously, this is the premier hatch of the early summer, overshadowing any other mayfly. Oh, by the way, there are also gray drakes hatching at the same time. Don't tell anybody. The numbers of both these monstrous insects seem to be on the rise. I hope they will also increase on the North Platte so a major hatch can occur on a yearly basis.

As summer enters the month of July, the pale morning dun makes its appearance, along with the sometimes blizzard hatches of caddis. Dry-fly fishing is good, and more of the upper river becomes fishable. The flows in the upper river have slowed enough for a fisherman to fish all the pocket water. The overall fishing is good, and the angler could choose the type of water he likes to fish.

This is a great time to take a backpack trip down the trail that runs from Hog Park to the Oddfellows camp. Here the fishing is not hatch-matching; general all-around dry flies and nymphs work well in the pocket water found upstream. The fish are smaller on average but fun nevertheless. It's a great way for a father and son or daughter to spend a few days: the hiking is not difficult and the fishing is relatively easy. Another option for July is to spend some time fishing Hog Park Creek, which is a very small tailwater. There are some mayflies hatching, but mostly one can expect to see caddis hatching out. The fish are small, but there is an occasional fourteen-to-sixteen-inch fish to keep things interesting.

The end of July and August is a time when the fishing on the lower section tends to slow down. There are some PMDs available and some

Late summer on the lower section.

real good evening caddis fishing for the egg-laying and diving caddis as they return to the water. But the overall fishing will have slowed. The larger fish seem to have disappeared from the river—most probably the warmer temperatures send them back to the small reservoir and deep holes. The upper river still offers good fishing, as does Hog Park Creek. Terrestrials account for a good deal of the resident fishes' diet. Ants, beetles, and small crickets should be fished at this time for success. The water levels have dropped in the upper portion, making for shallow areas interspersed with pools and small pockets. A little more care in the approach needs to be taken to make effective presentations to wary fish.

Fall (September, October, and November)
The cool, crisp days of autumn find the river very fishable. There may still be some spotty caddis, and the little *Baetis* mayflies begin to appear but, much like the spring and early summer, there are no great hatches. Fishing is limited to general searching patterns, nymphs, and

streamers. The brown trout begin feeding activities in earnest as spawning urges befall them. The lower section of river will find some decent-sized brown trout. Working the deeper water with weighted streamer patterns is often very effective.

The upper river is still good in the early part of fall, but as the days shorten and the nights get increasingly colder, the fishing gets spottier. Places where good numbers of fish are caught may not hold fish a week later. The fish begin to pool up or move downstream to the lower river in preparation for the long winter ahead. The colder water slows their metabolism down so they will not move to an imitation that is too far away from them. Presentations should be made very close, often on their noses, to be effective. Sometimes this can be accomplished at this time of year by sight-fishing to holding fish. A great deal of stealth is needed because the water is low and extremely clear and any overt movement will send the fish swimming to cover. The easy fishing of the summer months is effectively over. Actually locating fish can be a problem that only gets compounded by the need for accurate presentations to wary fish.

If the weather holds in the upper river, then Hog Park Creek can offer some interesting fishing. The little brook trout that reside in the creek and the ones from the Encampment will be looking to spawn. They become aggressive and are not above feeding heavily on anything presented to them. These fish are not very large, eight inches being the average, but they are beautifully colored. The fish in Hog Park Creek are interesting because some of these brookies are fully matured fish, though only eight inches long. Again, if redds are seen, pass on these fish—their lives are tough enough. These little brook trout spawn later in the fall than do the brown trout, often into December. Snows come and prevent access to the area more often than not.

Winter (December, January, and February)

Not much is open during the winter months because the waters are ice-choked. The only shot an angler has at catching any fish is to snowmobile into the Hog Park area and fish the tailwater near the dam. This water remains open but is very cold. This type of fishing is only for the angler with too much time on his hands.

Locally Effective Patterns

Green Drake Nymph

Hook: 8-12
Thread: Black, brown, olive
Tails: Pheasant-tail fibers
Ribbing: Copper wire
Abdomen: Peacock herl
Wingcase: Pheasant tail (dark side)
          tied over thorax
Thorax: Peacock herl
Legs: Fibers from wingcase tied
          back along the thorax

Green Drake Spinner

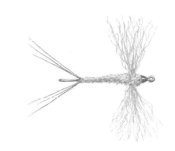

Hook: 10-12
Thread: Brown
Tails: Blue dun Micro Fibetts,
          split and divided
Body: Rusty brown dubbing
Wings: Gray Z-lon

Extended-Body Green Drake Dun

Hook: 10-12
Thread: Olive
Tails: Olive deer-hair fibers
Ribbing: Pearl Flashabou
Abdomen: Extended monofilament
          body dubbed with olive
          dubbing
Thorax: Olive dubbing
Wing: Clump of olive deer hair
          clipped into wing shape
Hackle: Olive-dyed grizzly tied
          parachute-style

Extended-Body Gray Drake Dun

Hook: 10-12
Thread: Gray
Tails: Natural deer-hair fibers
Ribbing: Pearl Flashabou
Abdomen: Extended body tied on
           monofilament, dubbed with
           medium gray dubbing
Thorax: Medium gray dubbing
Wing: Clump of natural deer hair
           clipped to wing shape
Hackle: Grizzly tied parachute-style

Other Effective Patterns

Adams
Elk Hair Caddis
Ginger Quill
Black gnat
Mosquito
Pale Morning Dun
Humpy
Coachman Trude
Renegade
Foam beetle
Letort Cricket
Ant (black, red)

Gold-Ribbed Hare's Ear
PMD nymph
Halfback
Prince Nymph
Platte River Carey
Bead Head Caddis
Peeking Caddis
Emergent Caddis
Blue Dun
Blue-Winged Olive
Woolly Worm
Woolly Buggers (black, olive)

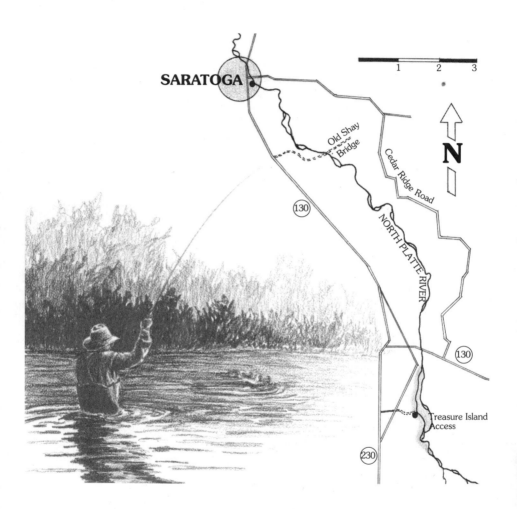

SARATOGA

Old Shay
Bridge

Cedar Ridge Road

NORTH PLATTE RIVER

130

130

Treasure Island
Access

230

N

1   2   3

5

The Encampment River
to Saratoga

This is perhaps the most popular stretch of water for the recreational floater as well as for the float fisherman. The river's proximity to the town of Saratoga and the ease of shuttling vehicles makes it relatively simple to float for the day or a few hours. The convenience of having a motel room, restaurant, or bar waiting at the end of a long day on the water also adds to this section's appeal.

Even though this is the most popular stretch, the crowds are manageable. Probably the busiest day of the year on the water is the Fourth of July, and it doesn't even come close to the flotillas encountered on a regular basis on rivers like the Big Horn, the lower Green, the Madison, and the Yellowstone. I imagine that as more and more fishermen become aware of the quality of fishing here, the pressure will increase.

The Saratoga area has always been a minor destination spot for sportsmen and vacationers, most of whom come from the Front Range of Colorado. The nearby scenery is gorgeous, the town offers the creature comforts, and the atmosphere is laid back and relaxing. The affluent have discovered Saratoga as a place to escape the pressures of career or fame. Over the Labor Day weekend, the number of private jets sitting on the airport runway is astonishing.

With all this and a wild trout fishery that boasts over 4,600 trout per mile without the pressure from swarms of anglers, what more can a fisherman ask for? The fishing here is as good as anywhere in the country, and the best part is that an angler can have quality fishing without leaving town—the river runs through it.

In the very recent past a large majority of anglers here were spin fishermen, but times are changing, and the move is to fly fishing. Many

69

of the local anglers are still spin fishermen, but they generally fish the high-water period between June and July 4 and look elsewhere when the water begins to drop. Fly-fishing pressure on the river by local anglers is practically negligible—this is not a very populated area. Fly fishermen here are becoming more sophisticated in the techniques they employ, and in their thinking: "catch and release" are no longer just words on a bumper sticker.

Topography

The river flows through the scenic Saratoga Valley—scenic in an understated way. The mountains that surround the valley are not the dramatic kind like the Tetons or Absarokas; they are simply there. To the north is Elk Mountain, the quiet sentinel of the valley, and to the south are the mountains of the Medicine Bow National Forest. As one approaches the river the alpine vegetation gives way to the range grasses and sagebrush that cover the hillsides. The riparian vegetation is a dense screening of cottonwood, willow, dogwood, and wild roses.

The river widens in this section and braids around many vegetated islands as it flows through the ranchland in the valley. Irrigated hay fields are common along the river. Mosquitoes are endemic to irrigated fields and can often be a problem on the water. Immediately after runoff some of the standing pools of water hatch out enough mosquitoes to make life miserable on windless days. Don't forget the repellent when fishing this area. There have been some float trips when the wind wasn't blowing when it seemed as if swarms of mosquitoes were drifting along with the boat. It's not often that a fly fisherman prays for wind, but these are certainly some of those times.

Water Characteristics

A characteristic that separates this portion of the river from the water upstream is the amount of braiding here. Instream islands force the river to split and divide around them and form various-sized channels. This makes for some super water to fish—as currents come back together they do so at different rates of speed. These edges where the two currents meet make wonderful funnels for food, and trout will always be found there. The islands help create all kinds of water types, from riffles to channels to pools. This rich variety of water offers the trout a selection to suit their needs, whether those be for feeding lies or holding lies.

The riffle-to-pool ratio is excellent in this stretch, thanks to the islands. Water depth varies from the extremely shallow to the very deep holes, and especially so over the course of a year as the flows and levels change. Undercut banks are prominent and provide the trout with good habitat. The dense riparian vegetation provides cover and some structure. The banks all have pockets that hold fish, especially in high-water conditions. There are some sections that have instream boulders that also provide cover and feeding lanes. The bottom is made up of different-sized rocks, but fist-sized rubble is the most characteristic bottom type. Since the gradient here isn't as steep as for upstream waters, there are areas that have a silty bottom, especially in the backwaters and eddies.

Some small tributaries empty in the river in this section, and some irrigation water spills back. It seems that these always have a few fish holding at their mouths that are willing to be caught, particularly so if you happen to be the first to cast to them. There are a few bridges that cross the river, and they provide structure for the fish as well as some deep water where the pilings are. A "bridge fish" or two is always to be anticipated on a float.

Water speed varies along this stretch, but it never seems real slow, even in low water. During the runoff period and immediately after, the water moves along at a pretty good clip. Although there are no white-water areas, floaters need to take some precautions. I have seen drift boats smashed up into the banks where the river makes a sharp turn. I guess the boaters weren't paying attention, and the force of the current pushed them onto the bank with enough force to fracture fiberglass hulls. I have also seen aluminum canoes wrapped around bridge pilings. This is not tricky or dangerous water, even during the high-water period, but every year there are some severe accidents that probably could have been avoided. As one enters Saratoga along the golf course, there is a series of waves that can swamp a boat when the water is high and boaters are not paying attention. And sweepers, trees or branches that hang over the water, are a potential hazard for the unsuspecting boater. It's easy to become engrossed with something else: looking for rising fish, watching your partner fight a fish, or staring at the recreational floaters.

Accessibility

This twelve-mile stretch of river flows through mostly private land and creates a good news-bad news situation regarding access. The good news is that there are about two miles of river that are accessible, and the bad news is that this land is concentrated at the beginning of the section. There is access at the end of the section, but it is confined to the town of Saratoga. The entire middle ten miles are private and inaccessible without violating trespass laws or seeking landowner permission. In order to fish the middle section, a float trip is necessary. This does create a problem in the middle of summer when the flows are low, because then it can take most of the day to float. And in order to stop for a rest or lunch, let alone to fish a pod of heavily working fish, a law must be broken. Some sort of access, even if it's only accessible to boaters, is dearly needed on this stretch.

The Treasure Island access, locally called Platuka or Baldwin's, is as good an access as there is in the state. It's easy to get to, with a paved highway leading to it, and it's just a short hop from town. There is a large parking area, so a boat owner can comfortably turn his rig around. Overnight camping is allowed, and there are toilet facilities. The ramp to the river is dirt but in good shape—two-wheel-drive vehicles can easily negotiate it without fear of getting stuck. When the water is low, the drift-boat owner might have to drag his boat to the far channel before he can find enough water to float. One year I ended up backing my trailer halfway across the river so I wouldn't have to drag it. This doesn't happen very often, though.

Treasure Island is a huge island, about two miles long, that divides the river into two channels. The access is on the west side at the approximate halfway mark. There is a wooden sign that depicts the boundaries, so an angler will not have to guess if he is breaking access laws or not. A trail runs upstream from the access point and crosses onto the island via a footbridge. An angler can find all kinds of water to walk-fish in either channel.

Something to consider when floating from an upstream section to this one is to remember to take the left, or west, channel. Some of my friends have forgotten to take the correct channel and had to float an additional twelve miles to take their boat out, then they had to hitchhike to Treasure Island to get their vehicle. It made for an overly long float and a group of crabby folks.

The next access point is town, and I guess one could say that this is the best access in the state. There is a concrete ramp, wonder of wonders, with ample parking across from it. Hot pools are right down the street in one direction, and a fly shop is in the other. Nothing compares to ending a float in town, especially if a shuttle has already been made and your vehicle is there waiting for you. The convenience of not having to drive anywhere to get to motel, restaurant, or tavern makes it very pleasant. Every time I float this stretch and end up in Saratoga I find it hard not to stop by the Wolf Hotel for a beer or two. Shuttle services are available through a few of the fly shops at reasonable rates.

There is some decent fishing to be had right in downtown Saratoga. Some of the bigger fish in the river are taken in town and, to add insult to injury, some huge fish are caught right behind one of the fly shops. Natural hot springs empty into the river and keep it open and fishable in the winter months. Saratoga advertises itself with the slogan, "Where trout jump in Main Street." After all, this *is* Blue Ribbon water. The local Trout Unlimited chapter, Platte Valley TU, is working with the town to clean up some of the more unsightly areas to provide for a more visually appealing fishing experience.

Management Practices

The section of river from Saratoga upstream is managed under the wild trout concept, and a slot limit is in effect. An angler may keep six trout, but all trout between ten and sixteen inches must be released, and only one may be twenty inches or larger. Fishing is permitted with flies or artificial lures only. Since the inception of the slot limit, the population of trout per mile has shown a dramatic increase. To my way of thinking, this section of river has to be a showcase for the success of a management philosophy. These special regulations may exclude some anglers who want to keep some fish for dinner from this section, but with so much other water close by, very few complaints are heard.

Larger fish than in the upstream section of the river are more evident here, probably because the habitat is more suitable. Fish in the five- to seven-pound range are caught in this section every year—not in great numbers, but often enough to keep an angler expectant. Big fish always seem to get hooked when an angler least expects them to and make for great "the one that got away" stories. Many of the local fishermen believe the recent low-water years have resulted in slightly larger and healthier trout because the fish haven't had to spend a great deal of time fighting the normally heavy runoff period. A rainbow trout's life span is normally about four or five years, and some of these fish are living their entire lives in low-water conditions, so maybe the lack of strain is paying off. Brown trout can live to be eight to ten years old and have also benefited from the easier flows.

It is usual in this section for the average brown trout to be larger at a given age than the average rainbow trout. After the age of three, browns seem to grow more in length each year than do rainbows. Studies have shown that browns in this section eat more Plecoptera species than do rainbows. Rainbows take a wider range of food items and are considered to have more generalized feeding habits than browns. Brown trout make greater use of forage fish (primarily longnose dace and suckers) in their diets, as much as four times more than rainbows. And browns become more specialized in their feeding habits as they grow larger. They appear to seek out the larger food items than do rainbow trout, which might account for their faster growth rates. The selection of different food categories by each of the species may be a mechanism to reduce competition for available food sources.

Some other generalizations about the feeding habits of brown and rainbow trout are of interest to the angler. The smaller trout of both species, those less than about eight inches, use far fewer categories of food items than do the larger fish. Trout in the eight- to twelve-inch range demonstrate a more generalized feeding habit and take a wide variety of food items. This suggests that this size group should be the most common in the fishing harvest. The angler that prospects with attractor-style flies, randomly fishing a section of water without specifically imitating a food item, will probably catch smaller fish than the angler that specifically attempts to imitate a food item. I seem to catch more small fish when I am just blindly fishing, especially when floating, than when I am matching a hatch or fishing to specific fish.

After trout reach a length greater than about twelve inches, they usually become more selective in their feeding habits, especially the brown trout. This can account for a phenomenon that local fishermen believe takes place in this section. Pods of similarly sized fish seem to feed in given areas. One day an angler might find a pod of smallish fish feeding at a location, and the next day the fish may be significantly larger in the same place. A local adage is that when the larger fish are feeding, the smaller fish are elsewhere.

Seasonal Changes in Fishing

This free-flowing section of river is affected by the ravages of weather and the change in seasons. Winter brings the cold, snow, and ice that make fishing impractical if not impossible. However, there are hot springs that dump into the river in Saratoga and keep the water ice-free, so there are some fishing opportunities in town. The angler who finds himself in Saratoga during the winter months might consider bringing some fishing equipment. There are days when the wind isn't blowing and the temperatures are moderate that could actually be enjoyable fishing for a few hours. Besides, if one does get a chill, the Hobo Hot Pools are nearby to warm one's bones. Wild trout in the middle of winter in the middle of town has to be one of those "this is certainly different" fishing experiences.

Early, gradual warming trends usually bring a short period when the ice has melted off the river and the water is clear. Then, once runoff begins, the fishing shuts back down. However, there are periods during the runoff when the temperature drops in the higher elevations upstream and retards the flows, allowing the river to clear enough to fish. These periods are highly unpredictable, and in order to take advantage of them one has to be in the right place at the right time. Toward the end of the runoff period the water begins to clear, even though the flows are still high, and this marks the beginning of the real fishing season.

The high-water period is usually over by the Fourth of July, though this of course depends on the year. The recent droughtlike conditions in Wyoming have left the river lower and clearing earlier than normal. Often the river is totally fishable in May, and sometimes many local anglers will begin floating in early May. A good rule of thumb is to call the local shops for information in the early season, otherwise some awfully good fishing could be missed. This early-summer period is the

Fishing the high water.

best time to float because the flows are high enough to move a drift boat downstream at a good clip without a boatman having to drag it across riffles. Also, one doesn't have to float over water that should be fished; this is especially important in this stretch because of the limited access to a large portion of the river.

After the high-water period, the river begins to drop and becomes typical of the midsummer, ending the good float-fishing. This is the time of year when there are good hatches of insects and classic fly fishing begins. The various mayflies that hatch create situations where pods of rising fish become selective to them, and an angler then needs to match the hatch. The lower, clearer water makes floating a little more difficult, and an angler has to be aware of where he is floating. Water that holds fish needs to be identified so it is not floated over; fishing from the boat becomes more of a "fish in front of the boat" deal than before. This is a very good time for the walking fisherman to work the Treasure Island area.

Midsummer during exceptionally warm years can find the river with elevated water temperatures. When this happens, the fishing absolutely stinks. A few summers ago there was a period when the water temperatures would climb into the seventies and the fishing would totally shut down. The trout become stressed and just don't feed until the water cools down at night. Thanks to the fishing gods, cool rains came and lowered the water temperature, or the rest of the season would have been dismal if not dangerous to the fish.

Fall finds the river even lower, especially in the years when there is little precipitation during the summer months. The nights begin to get cooler and fish begin feeding heavily in preparation for the long winter months ahead. The brown trout begin their spawning routines, and pressure on the river becomes almost nonexistent as hunting season starts. I think this is one of the better times to fish the river: there is still enough insect activity to get fish rising, and there is very little competition from other fishermen. The days get nastier as the season progresses until the fishing finally shuts down. My guess is that most people quit fishing before the fish quit feeding. The cold and ice of the winter months complete the cycle.

Spring (March, April, and May)

Once the ice is off the river there is usually a period in March or April before the runoff starts in earnest that is fishable. The water will be low, clear, and cold. If the weather stays on the warm side, a float trip or two might be snuck in before runoff. A few years ago I received a call from a friend who happened to be passing through and wanted me to meet him in Saratoga to do some fishing. I knew the river in the Rawlins area was high and mucky, so I began making excuses. He began putting pressure on me and I began making up better excuses. Then he let it slip that he had been there for a few days and had fished every day. "How did you do?" I smugly asked, expecting him to say not very good or that he just caught a few fish. "Real good. The fishing has been excellent, the water is low and clear," he replied, and then as an afterthought, "Oh, I landed five fish over twenty-three inches long." I didn't believe him, figuring it to be a ploy to get me down there. I did meet him, and the fishing was really that good. Over the beers I had to buy him he chided me about not wanting to meet him, while I hung my head in shame and mumbled, "Next time, call me earlier."

Nymphing is the most effective technique at this time. The river bottom is covered with a variety of stonefly nymphs that are nearing maturity. The majority of them most likely belong to the Perlidae family, commonly called brown willow fly. These generally hatch out at the peak of the runoff, but the nymphs are available before that. It usually takes two or three years for them to develop fully, so they are available to trout all year long. The period prior to their emergence is marked by mass migrations to the shore, where they crawl out of the water to hatch. These migrations generally occur in the afternoon or evening, and trout do feed voraciously on them. This coincides nicely with the early-season fisherman's habits. It is usually too cold to be on the water early in the day, so one gets a later start and fishes into the afternoon.

Years ago, when I discovered these large numbers of stonefly nymphs were present, I used to kick-screen the bottom and save samples in tiny bottles. I would bring them home, set them in front of my tying bench, and try to devise a pattern to match them. I now have a box of stonefly nymph imitations that have to be seen to be believed; I get a chuckle every time I open it. Stonefly nymph imitations of every imaginable configuration, using every imaginable material and tying style fill it—don't all of us have fly boxes filled with prototype flies? The irony of it is that I was already using a pattern that was more effective than anything I came up with, at least in this section of water. A Halfback nymph still outfishes specific patterns at this time of year, so much so that I gave up trying to devise anything better. Those pretty woven-body flies are relegated to a bottom drawer with the hundreds of other flies I will never fish.

A Halfback in a #6 or #8 is as effective, if not more so, than any other pattern I have used. In all fairness, I will say that a George's Stone is a close second, especially the variation with the rubber legs, during the early part of the season. This pattern dead-drifted along the bottom is the technique to use. The lower flows of this period form the river into pocket-water-type holding areas that make it fairly easy for the fisherman to guess where there might be fish. Any of the deeper pools below a riffle will hold trout. Rainbows are getting ready to spawn and seem to need more oxygenated flows than do brown trout, so they usually hold higher in the riffles where the flows are faster. Both species will feed on these abundant stonefly nymphs, but the brown trout become selective to them.

There are other insect species that are also available to the fish at this time, and the trout will feed on them, although maybe not as heavily as they do on stonefly nymphs. Caddis larvae are reaching a size that make them a good food source for the fish, and some of the mayfly nymphs are beginning to mature. Any smallish Gold-Ribbed Hare's Ear-type pattern will take some fish. The green drake nymph is growing to a relatively large size as it matures. These nymphs are abundant in sections of this stretch of river, and fish do take them readily. Halfbacks in smaller sizes, about #12 or #10, are very effective. The angler who will slowly fish a streamer pattern along the bottom or in the riffles will also connect with a few fish. The longnose dace and sucker are getting ready to spawn, so their presence is a factor, particularly to the brown trout. Dace are common throughout all the riffles in this section, and this early-season period sees greater concentrations of them.

The slower sections of water will have some fish feeding on midges as they hatch. I have never witnessed a super midge hatch here, but I don't doubt that one does take place. Pods of fish will work an area with hatching midges. Tiny dry flies drifted drag-free will provide for some long-anticipated top-water action. My favorite pattern in this section is a #20 Griffith's Gnat. Look to the calmer water in the early afternoon when the water begins to warm slightly. I read in a study that rainbow trout make good use of Dipterans as a food item, more so than brown trout do.

Once the water begins to rise and discolors with the surge of runoff, the fishing is over for a while. Unique to this section is that when the temperature drops in the upstream section, the runoff slackens. Water levels can drop and clear enough to allow some fishing. This is strictly a hit-or-miss opportunity; an angler has to be there when it happens to capitalize on it. Depending on the year, the runoff could slacken and the water could begin to clear as early as the beginning of May. Normally this doesn't happen until sometime in June, but recent low-water years have found the river extremely fishable in May.

Early Summer (End of May to the Beginning of July)

This is definitely the time of year to float this section. When the flows are high and clearing, this twelve-mile stretch can be floated in half a day. It probably is the busiest time on the river because most of the local spin fishermen are out floating: it's the time when they do extremely well. They are more able to get their offerings down to where the fish are and keep them there than a fly fisherman is during high, fast flows.

Every river seems to have a type of boat that is most common to that river. The Yellowstone River in Montana is probably the place for full-dress, large drift boats; other rivers will see mostly rafts, and the North Platte has mostly johnboats. Spin fishermen are probably responsible for the large numbers of johnboats on the river. These boats are fairly stable, have a shallow draft, and are very maneuverable. They provide a solid platform from which to sit and fish. Many of the local outfitters still use a type of johnboat, and many local fly fishermen still fish from one. They are convenient and can be stacked atop one another to fit on the same trailer.

But times are slowly changing. Drift boats are becoming more and more numerous on the river. Many of the local guides have one, and some of the outfitters have a few. They are simply more comfortable to fish out of for the fly fisherman. The spin fisherman can get away with a boat that doesn't lend itself to standing and casting, but the fly fisherman needs a stable platform with some bracing so he can stand and cast all day long. Drift boats may be a little heavier and harder to transport, but the overall comfort over the course of a day's fishing is hard to beat.

Twelve to eighteen inches of visibility means the river is fishable, so let the floats begin. The heavy flows have pushed the fish to the banks, where the water is slower and easier to hold in. There is also slightly more visibility along the banks than out in the main current. The fish are waiting for a food item to come drifting by. The job of the angler is to present his imitation in such a way that a fish can see it and has some time to eat it. This is easier said than done for a fly fisherman because of the effects of drag on his terminal tackle. Sinking-tip lines of at least 7-weight, short weighted leaders, and large patterns are essential for any chance at success. A variety of streamers and large attractor-style nymphs predominate as patterns of choice, with Woolly Buggers probably being the most popular. Black is the number-one choice, followed by olive. The Yellow and Black Bugger can outfish any other patern on any given day. Pure white, black-and-grizzly, and brown-and-yellow Buggers are also effective. Matuka-style streamers also have their days on the river. Nymphs like large Halfbacks, Montana Nymphs, Girdle Bugs, Yuk Bugs, and Bitch Creeks also do well.

Large cranefly (Tipulidae) larva imitations also do well, particularly when they are fished in the same manner as the other large nymphs and streamers. A #2 cranefly larva imitation fished at the end of a sinking-tip line can be deadly on certain days, outfishing everything else. These large wormlike creatures live under the gravel and silt in the river; the high flows of runoff dislodge them, causing them to tumble along the bottom in the current, where they become available to the trout. Normally, they would be fished dead-drift along the bottom, but here on the North Platte they are cast to the bank and allowed to swing in the current along the bottom or stripped back to the boat. They are very effective.

I used to think a great deal of flash should be added to patterns during the runoff period because the anglers fishing spinners did so well. So I began tying patterns that were almost entirely constructed of different colors and combinations of colored Flashabou. These patterns did not do any better than the Woolly Buggers and other relatively drab patterns. What was important was the way they were presented. They needed to get to the bottom quickly and stay there for as long as possible. This led to a slight change in my fishing technique from the boat.

Usually when one fishes streamer-type patterns from a boat, a cast is made to the bank and the fly is stripped back. This works fine some of the time, such as when the pattern falls into a pocket that is holding a trout and the fish immediately takes it. The banks that have deep water (greater than a foot) will have fish holding along the bottom, and the fly will generally be pulled away from the fish too quickly for it to react. The fly needs to spend some time sinking to the fish before it starts to move away from it. Think of it as a natural food item tumbling along in the drift, then suddenly coming to life. What trout could resist such an enticement? If the fly is then pulled up and away in the current, it more than likely will be refused, but if it moves away along the bottom, then it will more than likely be taken by the trout even if the fish has to move into the current a little way.

The alteration in technique is to cast either perpendicular to the bank or slightly to the upstream side of perpendicular. Then allow the boat to pull the fly from the bank—do not start stripping it back. Sometimes an upstream mend is necessary to allow the fly time to get to the bottom. If the current happens to be faster along the bank than it is by the boat, then a downstream mend may be necessary. The technique resembles trolling from the boat immediately before the line is picked out of the water for a new cast. This technique has been highly effective here and on other rivers where the presentation needs to be on the bottom. An added enticement is the addition of a large nymph on a short dropper about a foot and a half in front of a streamer. This "chaser" rig resembles a baitfish chasing a nymph and seems to trigger a reflexive strike from trout.

Another very effective technique, especially for anglers who don't own or don't want to mess with sinking-tip lines, is to dead-drift nymphs from the boat. This is best accomplished with a floating line, a longish leader (I prefer weighting the leader with split shot above the fly to weighted flies), and large strike indicators. The large strike indicators serve two functions: they act as a visual reference to detect a strike and measure the speed of the drift; and, more importantly, they keep the fly-line tip from sinking. Basically, they help keep the leader more vertical in the water column instead of at an angle along the bottom. I believe the angler will have more control over the fly if the leader is as vertical as possible.

The fisherman should cast to the downstream side of perpendicular to the bank, in front of the boat. As much of the floating fly line should be kept off the surface as possible or mended back upstream so that the fly is given a chance to sink. The angler should continually mend the line back upstream without disturbing the drift of the fly and leader based on the speed of the strike indicator. If the strike indicator is moving faster than the current, it is dragging, and a mend should be made to slow it down. A perfect speed is slightly slower than the current speed. The current along the bottom of the river is always slower than the surface current, probably because of the effects of friction. If the speed cannot be slowed by mending the fly line, then more weight should be added to the leader.

This is a very good technique for working pockets of water, current edges, and structure out in the current. The key is to remember that the artificial should be dead-drifted along the bottom at about the same speed as the rest of the material along the bottom. A presentation that moves faster than the rest of the material on the bottom, moves up and away from the bottom, or isn't within six inches of the bottom will not be as effective and may result in a long fishless day.

As the season progresses, the water begins to drop and clear up, but it is still moving at a good clip. The water may become too shallow along the banks for the heavy stuff, and the sinking-tip rigs may begin snagging the bottom more often than not. The dead-drift nymphing technique will still be effective in the deeper water along the banks and in the instream structures, but it will be less effective in the shallower areas. Of course, some adaptations to the setup could be made, such as moving the indicator closer to the fly, but this might involve constant fiddling instead of fishing. It is time to switch techniques.

Trout will continue to hold along the banks because the current is still strong enough to push them there and keep plenty of food items drifting by. A couple other things begin to happen that help dictate a switch in techniques: caddis are beginning to hatch, and the larger stonefly nymphs are moving or have moved toward the shore to hatch out. Some of the stoneflies have already hatched and the adults become available to the trout, often falling from bushes, being blown onto the surface, or becoming trapped in the surface as they lay their eggs. It is time to fish an attractor dry and attractor nymph setup. This entails a large attractor dry fly like a Stimulator, Royal Trude, Madam X, or such in about #10, heavily dressed with floatant. The attractor nymph should be a lightly weighted Halfback, Bitch Creek nymph, or a variation tied with the same colors but in the style of a Girdle Bug. The dry is tied to the end of the tippet and the nymph is tied on a piece of tippet material about two feet long and attached to the bend of the dry fly's hook (see drawing on page 127). The dry serves two functions: first, it is fished in the same manner as a dry fly—drag-free; and second, it serves as a strike indicator for the nymph. It aids in the detection of a strike on the nymph, aids in the measurement of the speed of the drift, and actually buoys the nymph. The nymph should be weighted but not so much as to continually pull the dry fly under the surface.

Cast this setup to the banks and control the line so that the presentation is made as one would a dry fly. Most likely, the casts will be made in front of the boat, on the downstream side, and mends will be made in the fly line to keep the drift drag-free. It is an extremely effective technique for this time, and even when the water drops to midsummer levels.

Toward the end of the high-water period caddis start to emerge, and a floating fisherman will encounter hatches. A good technique is to set up the terminal tackle the same as for the attractor dry and nymph but to use an Elk Hair Caddis as the dry and a soft-hackle fly as the nymph. This way casts can be made to feeding fish and both the adult and emerger are covered. If the setup does begin to drag, the soft-hackle will imitate an emergent pupa. This is good for the float fisherman who cannot get out of the boat or who doesn't have time to stop and work a group of fish. It also makes for an effective searching rig as one drifts down the river: casts can be made to the bank or any other good-looking water, and riffles can be covered before the boat enters them.

As the water begins to drop to the midsummer levels, more insect activity is apparent and it is once again time to change tactics. Many of the tactics discussed so far are effective during the lower flows; patterns may need to be altered to match the hatch. Matching the hatch becomes the name of the game in midsummer.

Midsummer (July and August)

This is the time of plenty, when the living is easy and the trout are fat and happy. Insects are in the air, the breezes are warm, and the fly fisherman can don a pair of shorts and wading shoes to do some wet wading in pursuit of a few fish. Float trips in this section of river take more time, but the weather is usually pleasant and it's great to be outdoors. There are plenty of classic hatches for the angler to hone his skills on, and there is excellent fishing to be had.

First and foremost among the species of insects available to the trout now is the caddis. These insects are probably the most consistently abundant in this section and are responsible for a great deal of enjoyment on the part of the fly fisherman. I find the caddis hatches to be fun to fish: trout are more flamboyant in their feeding displays, and the fishing is not as technical as it is for other hatches. An angler can be a little sloppier in his presentation and with the patterns he uses. The faster water of the riffles where the caddis normally hatch out is a contributing factor. The trout do not have the time to drift with an imitation, closely examining it before deciding whether or not to eat it. The broken water of the surface does not enable a fish to see the pattern for long distances. It is there, then it isn't—eat it or lose it.

The caddis pupa ascends to the surface rather quickly, where it emerges into an adult and generally flies off, often with false starts or a fluttering run. This is good news to the fly fisherman because it means that even if his pattern is dragging on the surface there is a good chance it will get eaten. Maybe the dragging fly imitates the fluttering or running actions of the adult, or maybe it is imitating an emergent caddis—it doesn't really matter as long as it is taken. The caddis pupa does rise to the surface fairly quickly, but as often as not it does so with a number of false starts. It may rise, then sink, then rise again until it finally reaches the surface to emerge into an adult. This rising action can be imitated with a soft-hackle, a wet fly, or a specific pupa pattern fished in a number of ways. The imitation could be dead-drifted along the bottom until the end of the drift, where it will rise to the surface because of the effects of the current pushing it up. If this can be timed so that it rises in front of some holding fish, then chances are one of them will take it.

Another technique that is effective is to allow the pupa imitation to sink to the bottom, then as it drifts downstream make a series of lifts with the rod tip to imitate the rising and falling action of a natural making false starts. This action could trigger strikes from trout anywhere in the drift. Perhaps the simplest technique is the classic wet-fly swing: cast either directly across-current or quartering downstream and allow the fly to swing with the current until it is directly downstream from your position. At that point, raise and lower the rod tip a few times before recasting. Trout can strike anytime during the drift, and many fish will be caught at the end of the swing when the rod tip is raised and lowered.

Knowing that there are plenty of caddisflies around could solve the "What fly do I use" problem for the nymph fisherman. The predominant caddis in this section of river are the Hydropsychidae and *Brachycentrus* species. The Hydropsychidae larvae do not build cases and can range in color from tan to green, while the *Brachycentrus* larvae do build cases out of plant fragments or sand grains. A Gold-Ribbed Hare's Ear nymph and the Red Fox Squirrel Nymph are as good as any patterns for imitating the Hydropsychidae, and a Herl Nymph or Zug Bug will do the trick for the *Brachycentrus.* Other, more specific patterns also work well as long as they fit the #10 to #16 size range.

One pattern style that has been very effective is the Bead Head. This relatively new pattern is distinguished by the large gold or brass bead on the head. The hook actually passes through the bead, and the body can be tied in any color to match the naturals. This pattern is an extremely hot fly on this river, as is the case with most good new patterns: they seem to be dynamite until most of the fish see them on a regular basis.

When the hatch does get going, usually somewhere around eleven in the morning, some of the patterns that imitate the pupa, like the various colored soft-hackles, LaFontaine's Emergent Sparkle Pupa, and the Olive K-Flash Caddis Emerger, are very effective. The adults can be imitated with Elk Hair Caddis, Bucktail Caddis, Humpies, and a variety of Trude patterns.

The late afternoon and evening bring swarms of mating caddis back to the water, where they lay their eggs. Some dip and dap their abdomens into the surface of the water, and others actually dive into the water, lay their eggs along the river bottom, and swim to the surface and fly off. This is a good time to fish soft-hackles, wet flies, or diving caddis patterns in the riffles. Most caddis will return to the riffle they hatched from to lay their eggs; this probably insures the propagation of the species.

In the early part of this midsummer period, an angler may run across sections of water that have some very good *Baetis* species, little blue-winged olive, hatches. These early hatches aren't as thick and strong as the fall hatches, but fish can be found feeding on these small mayflies.

They hatch out of the riffles about the same time as the caddis do, but the trout look to other types of water to feed on them—maybe their size plays a role here. The calmer, quieter water is where an angler can expect to find fish feeding on *Baetis*. Look to the back-eddies, the flat water along the banks, along the inside bends of riffles, to the edges of pools, and to the tailouts.

A floating fisherman might find it difficult to make decent presentations to these fish because of the motion of the boat. Drag-free presentations are essential, and the fisherman in a boat will find that there are fish working in the slower water where he could pull the boat over. This is a tough situation. I find that by casting as far in front of the boat as one can and still be accurate, I can take some of these feeding fish. The fly and leader will float to the fish before the line, and I can sometimes manipulate the fly into the feeding lane of the fish. Trouble is, if the currents are varied between the boat and fish, it could be real difficult making a presentation. The fish holding against the bank are the tough ones because the cast has to be accurate to start with. There will be little time to make any adjustments before the fish are spooked— they will see you coming.

Long, accurate casts are a tough row to hoe for the novice fly fisherman. I usually attach a small soft-hackle on a two-foot piece of tippet to the bend in the dry fly's hook. Many fish will take the soft-hackle even if it does drag a bit. This makes it a little easier for the beginner and is a great way to cover tough fish in tough places from the boat. The wading angler can fish in the classic dry-fly style and can make his presentation without factoring in a moving boat to the equation.

Effective patterns that imitate the dun include: tiny Blue-Winged Olive, Blue Dun, small Adams, and Blue Quills, all about #18 or #20. The soft-hackle has an olive body, copper ribbing, and partridge hackle. After throwing big stuff in the early season, these tiny flies take some getting used to. But it's just a matter of time.

There are other hatches of mayflies, but they are not great hatches, and most aren't even good hatches. They hatch out in small numbers or as onesies and twosies, are very sporadic, and are hard to find consistently. Fish do take them, most probably opportunistically, so the angler can use other mayfly patterns to fish blind, or to search with, and expect some success. Some of the other mayflies that can be found in this section of river but do not inspire feeding binges are: gray drakes (*Siphlonurus* species), great western lead-wings (*Isonychia* species), green drakes (*Ephemerella* species), blue quills (*Paraleptophlebia* species), march browns (*Rhithrogena* species), and the little yellow may (*Epeorus* species). An angler may happen upon an area where one species of these mayflies is hatching in good numbers, so he should be prepared; most likely it will be the wading fisherman who has the time to identify it. The float fisherman will see some bugs on the water, see fish rising, and be gone before any identification can be made, especially if the hatch is very light.

A premier mayfly that hatches out in numbers great enough to make the fish crazy is the pale morning dun. Dark overcast days or better yet drizzly days see the best hatches, and sometimes they are blanket hatches. The hatches are fairly consistent and the fish do key to them. The PMD nymph is short and stocky in shape and becomes active during the preemergence period of midmorning. Around eleven o'clock they begin rising to the surface to emerge into duns. The duns float on the surface before flying off to the bushes to escape the dehydrating effects of the sun and to evolve into spinners. Mating occurs in swarms, then the females return to the water to lay their eggs. Both males and females fall to the water as spentwings. All stages of this insect's life cycle are important to the trout and hence to the fly fisherman.

The trout do get on the nymphs as they become active prior to emergence. A specific #16 PMD nymph imitation or a stocky-bodied Hare's Ear will do well. As more of these nymphs rise from the bottom, some of the fish will begin taking the emergers. These are difficult fish to spot because much of their feeding activity is below the surface. A good way to cover these fish is to dead-drift the nymph in the regular fashion and then, as the current pulls it toward the surface at the end of the drift, either quickly lower the rod tip or let some slack line go from your hand. This might imitate the false starts many nymphs make as they rise to the surface. An angler could use a soft-hackle pattern dressed in the colors of a PMD nymph and fished on a wet-fly swing if he wanted to, especially if it is apparent that the trout are keyed to this stage.

Sooner or later the trout will look to the surface for the nymphs that are actually emerging, the duns or insects that are trapped in the surface film like cripples. A pattern that very effectively imitates the emerger and the cripple is the Para-tilt, also known as the Quigley Cripple. This pattern floats in the surface film so that its body hangs at an angle under it; the parachute hackle suspends it and the deer-hair wing sticks straight up out of the water. It resembles a dun climbing out of its nymphal shuck and a dun trapped in the shuck. This pattern is fished like a dry with a drag-free drift to visible fish in their feeding lanes. It is very effective.

The duns can be imitated with a zillion different patterns. I guess the one you use is dictated by how finicky the fish are or your personal choice. If the duns are on the surface of broken, riffly water I like to use a fully dressed pattern that is fairly heavily hackled so that it floats well and I can see it. If there are also caddis present, I like the PMD-caddis combination because this way I have a shot at taking fish eating PMDs or caddis. On the smoother sections of water I like a sparsely dressed thorax pattern with split tails. If the fish are very fussy, a Comparadun, Sparkle Dun, or No-hackle will usually fool them, provided the presentation is good. When fishing from a moving boat I like to combine a dun pattern with a soft-hackle so that, if I am a bit careless, I still have a chance.

Later in the day, toward the evening, the spentwings will be on the water and a Rusty Spinner will effectively imitate them. The problem is that this phenomenon never seems to be real heavy, so fish will not feed as if there were a hatch on. The calmer water will have fish that rise every so often in a random fashion—nothing patterned—and it is a good bet these fish are eating spent PMDs. These patterns lie flush in the surface film and can be difficult to see, so the addition of a mayfly dun pattern tied as a dropper above can act as a visual aid.

These patterns are especially difficult to fish from a moving boat. The fish hold in quiet water that has just enough current to bring the flies to it; this quiet water allows the fish to clearly see what is ahead of it. The high profile of a drift boat is hard to mistake and can put spooky trout down for the rest of the night. Long, accurate casts are imperative for any degree of success. Whether one is fishing from a boat or wading, it is important that the drifts be absolutely drag-free; after all, these bugs are dead and not likely to flutter about.

This is a funny section of river. One day a riffle wil have PMDs hatching and the next day there will be caddis. But you can bet your bottom dollar that if it is overcast and drizzly you will find PMDs in super numbers.

There is a wide variety of stoneflies available at this time, although they are few in number. There are goldens, little yellow sallies, and lime sallies. What this means to the angler is that he can use some larger patterns to prospect when nothing seems to be on the surface. The floating fisherman will find it refreshing to throw attractors into likely looking spots as he drifts by. More important to the angler is the knowledge that they are around, and so are nymphs. There will be many times between hatches or between pods of rising fish when there is nothing doing on the surface, so the angler has to go subsurface if he wants to consistently catch fish; he has to nymph-fish.

The availability of these stonefly nymphs makes his choice of flies easy. He can use a variety of stonefly patterns, but he will always catch fish on a Halfback. This is the bread-and-butter fly on this stretch of water. Combine a Halfback with a generic mayfly imitation as a two-fly rig and you can hardly go wrong.

One year I was fishing the Treasure Island section in the middle of the afternoon. Why, I don't know—I think it was because I was there. There wasn't anything going on so I thought I'd do some nymphing. I caught a few small fish and wasn't really into fishing when I thought I snagged on the bottom. I angrily pulled at the line to free it when I noticed that everything was moving downstream. "Geez, I hooked a tree limb and now freed it so it could drift in the current," I thought. So I grabbed the line with my hands and began pulling it back to me hand over hand. As this snag neared me, the water exploded and a brown trout that looked to be well over two feet long jumped in my face. After a flurry of moving arms and legs, I tried to get the fish back on the reel. I had to strip line like a madman to accomplish it, but I did and then promptly lost the fish. I felt stupid and looked around to see if anyone was watching. That brown trout took the small Halfback nymph with him and I went home.

Toward the end of this period, *Tricorythodes* species become the important mayflies. Clouds of swarming tiny insects can be seen along the shore in the morning hours. The spinner fall is the stage of most interest to the fisherman, and this occurs about nine o'clock and lasts until noonish or until the wind picks up and blows them off the water. The float fisherman will find it extremely difficult to fish these Tricos because the fish are holding in skinny water and are hard to approach from a boat. The patterns used to imitate them are so small that they are virtually impossible to see from long distances, and long casts are necessary from a boat. The Trico spinner fall is best fished by the wading fisherman.

The good news is that Treasure Island access has very good hatches of Tricos. The fish here hold and feed in water that is almost currentless— just enough to carry food to them. Presentations are the key to success. An errant presentation will be rewarded with a refusal, and even a good presentation might go unnoticed. Unlike other stretches of the river, where fish are not very pattern-conscious, these fish can be awfully finicky. A pattern that has worked well for me is a Cul de Canard spinner pattern. It is tied with four or five fibers from a white cul de canard feather for each wing. The natural oil in the fibers helps keep it afloat, and the feathers are wispy enough to resemble the delicate wings of a Trico spinner. Presentations need to be made exactly in the feeding lanes of these fish because they will not move even a few inches to take a fly. Because of the nature of the water that the fish hold in, it can be real tough getting close enough to make a good presentation. The disturbance of the water from wading can put the fish down, very often for good. Tiny flies, long delicate leaders, careful wading, and accurate presentations make this technical fishing, but it is very rewarding when one of these tough fish is hooked and landed.

Fall (September, October, and November)

Elk are starting to bugle in the surrounding high country and many of Wyoming's fishermen have other things on their minds: most antelope seasons are opening and the archery season has opened, as have the sage grouse and dove seasons. The river is left pretty much to the diehard anglers who have no interest in hunting. After the Labor Day crunch of visitors, campers, and recreational floaters, the river belongs to the serious fisherman. It takes a serious fisherman to float the river when the snow is falling, as it often does in the autumn, but the rewards are great.

The North Platte runs through the golden hues of the valley, and the fishing couldn't be better. The water is clear, the flows are low, and there are few people to contend with. Tricos are still going strong in early September but will begin to diminish in intensity as the month moves on. The trout, especially the browns, begin to put on the feed bag and seem to be a little more careless in their feeding habits. Brown trout once again become selective to the stonefly nymphs that are abundant on the stream bottom. They begin to change color as their spawning season approaches. The males also begin to stack up below some of the riffles as if they were waiting for some signal to spawn; this is a phenomenon I have noticed in many western rivers. Some riffles hold only males, and they are bunched together in a relatively small segment. The first spate of really nasty weather seems to trigger this behavior, and if it stays nasty the fishing could be awesome, but if the weather moderates the fish scatter back to their normal lies.

Nymph-fishing is excellent at this time of year, mostly because there isn't as much surface activity as there was during the summer months. There still are hatches that are quite good, but they aren't as plentiful and common as they are in the summer. Once the Tricos start to wane, the little *Baetis* species begin to pick up. The hatches occur later and later in the day in the autumn, probably because it takes longer and longer for the water to warm. There are still some caddis hatches, but these become a matter of being in the right riffle at the right time.

One late September I floated this stretch and had an average day—a few fish here and there but nothing terribly exciting. The wind picked up and it got chilly toward the late afternoon and I was about ready to call it a day when I floated over a riffle and, out of the corner of my eye, saw the flash of a fish rising. I pulled the boat over and watched, and sure enough another fish rose. I had an Elk Hair Caddis on, so I cast toward the fish and immediately hooked it. I finally had to leave the riffle after twenty-five fish because I didn't want to float the rest of the stretch in the dark. There were caddis hatching out of that riffle that afternoon, and I almost missed it. The caddis hatches are lighter and not as obvious as in the early season, and the angler needs to be on the lookout for them.

The *Baetis* is the important mayfly in the fall, and the hatches seem to be more intense than in the early part of the season. More importantly, there seems to be more mayflies around the water in the later afternoon and more fish seem to feed on them. The normal dry-fly patterns will all take fish, but I like to use a soft-hackle at this time of year. A great deal of fish seem to hold in the tailouts of pools and runs or in the slicker, flatter water, and a soft-hackle swung in front of them always seems to entice a strike. Even when I fish the traditional dry patterns, I still attach a soft-hackle and dare say that I catch the majority of fish on the soft-hackle.

The overcast days that spit snow seem to have the heaviest hatches, particularly so if they are also windless. One year I guided a couple of full-time guides from Idaho. They had heard about the fishing and were interested in catching a large brown trout. They could care less about catching regular-sized fish because they had just spent an entire season on the water catching normal fish almost every day. They wanted a big brown or nothing. It was a perfect day with perfect conditions for a large brown: dark and stormy with a light snow falling. Fishing was only fair, but a blanket hatch of *Baetis* species appeared on the water. Fish were feeding everywhere I looked, but these guys were nonplussed; they continued tossing large streamers in search of the big brown. I tried to get them to switch and catch some fish, but they were adamant about the brown. Finally one of them cracked and picked up his other rod. He put a Blue-Winged Olive dry and a soft-hackle on and was immediately into fish. After he landed a couple of fourteen-inchers he put his rod away and went back to throwing streamers. The other fellow never did break—he just kept tossing streamers. We never got into any big fish, but they didn't mind. They knew that if they fished the hatch they would have caught a ton of fish. It was a very weird day on the water, and the worst part was that I had to trailer my boat home to Rawlins in the snow.

Streamer-fishing is usually good at this time of year, and some very large fish are caught, but the water levels make it tricky. A good deal of water that should be fished has to be floated over. The boat should be pulled over before this type of water is reached so that a few casts can be made into it. Techniques are also different because of the shallower, slower water. A floating fly line and long leader are needed now. A heavily weighted pattern or split shot on the leader is also a requirement. I like to fish unweighted Woolly Buggers that have split shot pinched to the eye of the hook. This way, I can work the rod tip in a jigging action. If a nymph is attached to the leader on a dropper, current edges and holes can be worked by nymphing in the normal way and then

Winter fishing in town. (Photo courtesy Steve Hays)

letting the current swing the nymph and streamer downstream and working the streamer back with twitches or a jigging motion. This is an effective way to cover some of the shallower water in this stretch.

Overall, the fall has some very good fishing, and the nymph fisherman will consistently catch his share of fish. There is enough dry-fly action to satisfy the addict, and the streamer aficionado will have plenty to keep him occupied. The trout are fat and healthy, the water is not pressured, and life is good.

Winter

The river mostly shuts down during the winter months as it ices over. The angler with cabin fever can get out and fish for a few hours in downtown Saratoga. The hot pools keep sections of water ice-free in town, and some surprisingly good fishing can be had. There is some very good winter holding water there, the kind of water that is deep enough for trout to stack up in. The winter fishing is confined mostly to nymphing, and the angler with a #8 Halfback will find himself playing trout on Main Street.

This Blue Ribbon section of river is one of the most popular stretches and has some of the most interesting water. The average angler can come to the area to catch wild brown and rainbow trout, play some golf, take in a hot pool, do some sightseeing, and generally kick back and enjoy.

Locally Effective Patterns

George's Brown Stone Nymph (Rubberlegs)

Hook:	8-14
Thread:	Brown
Tails:	Dark brown mink guard hairs or tail
Abdomen:	Woven medium brown and tan yarn, brown on top
Thorax:	Dark brown mink fur with short guard hairs
Legs:	White oval rubber legs

Cranefly Larva

Hook:	2-8
Thread:	Gray
Body:	Lead wire overwrapped with light yellow floss, then wrapped with a mix of 20% light muskrat, 20% pale sulphur, and 60% olive hare's-ear dubbing

Bitch Creek–Girdle Bug Combo

Hook:	8-12
Thread:	Black
Ribbing:	Copper wire
Overbody:	Black chenille
Underbody:	Orange chenille
Legs:	Three pairs of white rubber legs

Olive K-Flash Caddis Emerger

Hook:	10-18
Thread:	Brown
Rib:	One strand of lime green K-Flash
Body:	Dark olive dubbing
Hackle:	Brown partridge
Antennae:	Three strands of lime green K-Flash

Baetis Soft-Hackle

Hook:	14-20
Thread:	Brown
Rib:	Copper wire
Body:	Olive dubbing
Hackle:	Brown partridge

Para-Tilt

Hook:	14-18
Thread:	Brown
Tails:	Bronze mallard flank
Ribbing:	Copper wire
Abdomen:	Pheasant-tail fibers
Wingcase:	Gray deer hair
Wing:	Gray deer hair; an extension of the wingcase ties at an angle tilting forward
Thorax:	Pale yellow or sulphur dubbing
Hackle:	Medium blue dun, parachute-style

Cul de Canard Trico Spinner

Hook:	18-24
Thread:	Black
Tails:	White hackle fibers, split and divided
Body:	Black, dark gray, or dark olive dubbing
Wings:	Four or five fibers from a white cul de canard feather

Other Effective Patterns

Woolly Buggers
  black
  olive
  yellow-and-black
  black-and-grizzly
  white
  brown-and-yellow
Matukas
Halfback
Girdle Bug
Yuk Bug
Bitch Creek Nymph
Stimulator
Royal Trude
Madam X
Gold-Ribbed Hare's Ear
Red Fox Squirrel Nymph
Herl Nymph
Zug Bug
Bead Head Caddis Larva

Platte River Carey
Soft-hackles
LaFontaine's Emergent Sparkle Pupa
PMD nymph
Comparadun
Sparkle Dun
PMD dun
Rusty Spinner
Elk Hair Caddis
Bucktail caddis
Diving caddis
Adams
Ginger Quill
Pale Evening Dun
Blue Dun
Blue Quill
Little Blue-Winged Olive
March Brown
Green Drake
Gray Drake

Pick Bridge Road

Pick Bridge Access

NORTH PLATTE RIVER

Easements

Foote Access

Jack Creek

1   2   3

N

130

SARATOGA

6

Saratoga to Pick Bridge

I always think of this section of river as a second cousin to the upper river. I know that many of the summer hatches are more intense below Saratoga, and I have had some phenomenal fishing here, but I always seem to float it as a second choice. Wind plays a big factor: There have been afternoons when I've had to turn my drift boat around and row for all I was worth downstream.

This is a very popular piece of water, especially so with the fishermen who want to keep some fish, because there is no slot limit to contend with. It is water that is easy to reach and handy to float. It also has some easements in the lower half where an angler can get out of the boat and wade. All in all, this piece of water offers convenience, variety, and some very good fishing.

Topography

The river here meanders through a transitional zone between the bottomland of the ranching community in the valley and the arid high plains farther downstream. Much of it still flows through ranching land, but there is more and more evidence of sagebrush creeping toward the water's edge. Sagebrush, willow, rose, and various grasses occur with stands of cottonwood to form a narrow band of riparian vegetation. The rolling hills away from the river are almost entirely sagebrush-covered and windswept. The river carves its way along relatively high bluffs in some sections. These sandstone formations create an odd backdrop and can create problems for the wading fisherman. Casting can be difficult from the bluff side because of the limited room for the backcast. These bluffs also seem to act as funnels for the wind.

Water Characteristics

Below Saratoga, the river is characteristic of most lowland floodplain waters, with a more gentle gradient and longer meanders. The river channel is composed of finer silts and more frequent sandbars than is the upstream stretch. A good deal of the fish cover is limited to deep holes and below the shallow riffles. There is a good deal of bank erosion, often with large sections of the bank fallen into the water. Many eroded sections have claimed the cottonwoods that were growing near the water's edge. The eroding banks may offer trout some temporary habitat; the clumps that fall into the water will very often have fish holding behind them or in the pockets they create, but the earth will eventually disintegrate and wash into the river. The banks will eventually degenerate and in effect widen the river and make it shallower. It is enough of a problem that the department of fish and game believes some reclamation and enhancement of trout habitat in the river through revetments on eroding banks and construction of habitat would improve the production of wild trout.

The entire stretch isn't in danger—there are areas of very good trout habitat. Undercut banks, deep holes, a good ratio of riffles to runs and pools, and some instream boulders all provide habitat for trout. There are many instream islands that cause the river to braid into smaller channels, offering a variety of water speed, depth, and current edges. Many of the high banks have deep water running along them and various pockets and structure that allow fish to hold and feel secure. The trees that have fallen into the river also provide cover, as does some of the overhanging vegetation. The abundance of riffled areas provides very good food-producing habitat, which probably accounts for the good hatches found in this stretch.

On the negative side, there are more areas that have slower flows and silty bottoms here than upstream. There is less of a large-rubble-bottom configuration and far less tributaries for spawning or nurseries. The only stream in this section that provides any spawning opportunities for trout is Jack Creek. The river itself here has less spawning habitat than upstream.

Accessibility

The float fisherman will find that he has more access options on this section of river. The upstream access is the town of Saratoga with its premier launch facility, and the downstream accesses are Foote (locally called Sheep Rock), which is a little over six miles away, and Pick Bridge at about eleven miles. A slightly shorter float is from Foote to Pick Bridge, which is about four and a half miles away.

There is a variety of water to float, so the angler with a boat can tailor the trip to suit his needs. There is a small easement upstream of the Foote access that is only legally accessible by boat. This is a convenient place to stop and fish or rest, especially if the longer float is chosen. Launch sites and take-outs are on the primitive side, with the exception of the Saratoga town ramp. They are usually nothing more than cuts in the bank so a boat can be dragged out or slid into the water. Very often these launch areas are severely rutted and muddy, so some care needs to be taken if your vehicle is a two-wheel-drive.

The walking fisherman has plenty of water to fish: there is about a mile of accessible water at the Foote site and all kinds of water at the Pick Bridge site. Most of the access at Pick Bridge is downstream of the bridge, but there is almost a mile of accessible water upstream, with an access road along the river. Both sites have good all-weather gravel roads leading to them and signs indicating where the roads are from the highway. However, the roads at the access sites that lead up- or downstream are not gravel-based and are in terrible shape. They are badly rutted, and if the weather dumps any kind of moisture on them they can be extremely slick. They are usually passable in dry weather, even in two-wheel-drive vehicles, but caution is advised in wet weather, and it is always a good idea to take your time.

Overnight camping is available at both sites. These campsites are really just areas where camping is allowed; they are not formal camping areas, and there is no fee. There is also no water supply, so the camper should bring what he needs. There are some primitive outhouse facilities. All of the fish and game access areas are under the "pack your own trash" system, which has seen good success.

Management Practices

The Saratoga Inn Bridge is the point that splits the river into two management-plan sections and provides for diversified fishing opportunities on the river system. Upstream of the bridge is the wild-trout slot-limit management plan that allows fishing with artificial lures and flies only. Downstream from the bridge to Interstate 80, the river is managed under the "Basic Yield Concept," where an angler can take six trout per day with only one twenty inches or better. Bait, including dead minnows, may be used. However, the Pick Bridge area is managed as a trophy area, and there is a slot limit in effect. Fish between ten and twenty inches must be released.

Trout are usually stocked under the Basic Yield Concept, but this section of the North Platte isn't. Most of the planting is done farther downstream, near the I-80 bridge. The trout population in this section is a result of fish drifting down from the upstream sections and of fish migrating upstream from the lower sections. The population is estimated to be lower in this stretch than upriver, but not by a lot. There is a slightly greater percentage of rainbow trout here because of fish moving up from Seminoe, especially so during some of the spawning periods. April is the time when rainbow trout attempt to spawn in this section of river, even though the natural spawning habitat is very limited, which restricts the natural reproduction. Jack Creek is the only tributary that is suitable for spawning.

Migration of walleye from Seminoe Reservoir into this section of the river is increasing with the growing population in the reservoir. Here they compete with trout for forage and prey on smaller trout, which could become a problem if their numbers increase. The principal forage for walleye is the longnose dace, which is also eaten by trout, particularly brown trout.

Seasonal Changes in Fishing

As the seasons change, so does the river. The ice of the winter melts, giving way to the runoff period. Prior to the runoff there may be a brief period when the river is fishable, but this is dependent on the weather. As the runoff tapers, the river is extremely fishable into the summer. Some years that are marked by low water and very high temperatures will cause the water temperature to rise into the seventies for brief periods and will shut down the fishing. When the river gets this warm, the only time that is even worth fishing is very early in the morning. The water temperatures in the evening are still too warm.

Midsummer brings low flows that are susceptible to changes in weather. Summer thunderstorms here or upstream can roil the water and put off fishing for a few days, but this section does clear rapidly. As the seasons move into fall, the river is at a lower level and very clear. Winter returns to shut out any fishing opportunities.

Spring (March, April, and May)

Sometime during this very early season is a period of clear water before the runoff begins in full force and after the ice is off the river. This happens for a short time almost every year, but if there are periods of rain or snow during this time the river may be unfishable. When the clear-water period actually happens is a function of a number of variables such as temperature, snowpack, precipitation, and groundwater saturation. Planning a trip to coincide with this time would be next to impossible. One year might find the river fishable in March, the next April, and the following year not at all. However, if an angler is anxious to get out and fish, a quick call to one of the fly shops in Saratoga will provide the needed information.

Whenever the river is clear enough to fish, some very good fishing can be had. There is a good supply of longnose dace for the streamer fisherman to imitate. The dry-fly enthusiast might find some of the slower sections of water with a moderate midge hatch, but most of the fish will be caught by the nymph fisherman.

There will be a wide variety of insects available on the stream bottom: the caddis larvae are nearing maturity, as are some of the mayfly nymphs, but the name of the game will be stonefly nymphs. There is a good assortment of species and sizes available, and the brown trout do selectively seek these food items. Most of the nymphs will be a variety of the Perlidae, or golden stone, that emerge in the spring and into midsummer. They can be found in sections of water that have graveled riffles and stony bottoms. They do get caught in the drift and during some periods migrate to the shore to crawl out and emerge into an adult. The nymph fisherman using a dead drift along the bottom will have good success.

Effective patterns include: George's Brown Stone Nymph (with or without rubber legs), Kaufmann's Brown Stone, Bitch Creek, Golden Stone, Yellow Stone Nymph, Montana Nymph, Sparkle Stonefly (an

Orvis pattern), Heartwell Stone Nymph, Black Rubberlegs, large Gold-Ribbed Hare's Ear, large Red Fox Squirrel Nymph, Brown Simulators, Whitlock Stonefly nymphs (brown, golden), and the ever-effective Halfback. My preference is the Halfback nymph in #6 or #8. It never seems to disappoint me.

A two-fly nymphing setup tied with a #14 cased caddis larva or a Gold-Ribbed Hare's Ear on the dropper with a Halfback as the point fly is an effective combination for this early period. Every fly fisher has pet patterns that imitate these particular insects, and most will work on this section of water as long as they are presented along the bottom. This may be a fairly popular stretch of river, but the fish never do get overly pressured, especially this early in the year. This is the time for the fly tier to test his prototype nymph patterns.

Once runoff starts in full force, the fishing is pretty much over until the river begins to clear again. There may be some very brief periods when the temperature drops and retards the runoff flows, but as one moves farther and farther downstream the likelihood of this happening grows less. Once the finer, siltier materials from the surrounding countryside begin to flow into the river it will stay murky and take longer to clear. Later in the spring, when the countryside begins to dry out, the water will begin to clear.

Early Summer (End of May to Beginning of July)

This is the period of fishable high water and strong flows. Twelve to eighteen inches of visibility is all that is needed to start. This is the time to be floating. The wading fisherman will have some difficulty with the strong flows, especially early in this period. It isn't impossible, but some careful planning is needed.

Some careful thought is needed to plan where to fish, what kinds of water are actually fishable with limited amounts of wading, and how not to become endangered while fishing. High flows will limit the wading angler's selection of water, but the water that he does find can be fished more slowly and thoroughly than by the floating fisherman. Riffles can be covered far better by a wading angler than by an angler in a boat. Trout during this time often will be feeding in riffled areas on the abundant longnose dace that get displaced by the stronger flows. Some very big fish come out of riffles in the early summer, but very few are taken by float fishermen. It is simply too difficult to cover a riffle with a streamer

Nymphing downstream of Saratoga. (Photo courtesy Steve Hays)

from a boat, and water that should be fished gets floated over in order to pull the boat into the slower water. Of course, if the riffle happens to be in one of the easements, the angler can pull the boat over and get out before he floats over it.

The floating fisherman will find some extremely good fishing by using the high-water techniques discussed in previous chapters. The only thing I do differently in this stretch is use a different streamer pattern. I like the Clouser Deep Minnow because it can cover the deep holes. The water takes on an almost pocket-water quality in certain sections, even during high water, because of the sharp twists and turns of the river. Water is presented to the angler very quickly, and it pays to get an imitation down to the level of the fish as fast as possible. The deeper, slower sections can be fished by imparting a jigging motion to the fly on the retrieve. Heavily weighted "bug" eyes quickly send a fly to the bottom, where an occasional walleye will be caught. The brown-and-yellow color combination fished in this jigging style imitates a crawfish. The other color combination I like to fish in this situation is olive-and-black.

This water also lends itself to nymphing from the boat with a large strike indicator and either heavily weighted nymphs or weight on the leader. Early in the period the big stuff is effective, and as the water clears and begins to drop, normal-sized nymphs can be used. The large Halfbacks, Bitch Creeks, and such are the ticket early on because they can be seen by the fish quickly and easily and there are still a great deal of natural stonefly nymphs available to the fish.

Once the water begins to clear, the attractor-dry-and-nymph combination is very effective. The water is still high enough for an angler to fish the banks, and the fish are still holding against the banks. The large attractor dry and a #10 lightly weighted Bitch Creek-Girdle Bug combination can bring fast and furious action. The more I fish with this setup the more I like it, although casting is a little weird. The dry fly tends to deceive the eye in judging distance, and the nymph often ends up being cast too long. There is also a hinging effect where the tippet with the nymph is tied to the dry, but the effectiveness of this system more than makes up for any of its shortcomings. All kinds of water can be fished as long as it isn't too deep: the banks, instream structure like boulders, various current edges, and pool tailouts. The edges between the fast and slow water of a riffle are particularly good spots to drop this combination into.

As water levels begin to drop, the wading fisherman can cover more water either with a streamer or by nymph-fishing. The caddis are starting to pop, and the little blue-winged olives are making their appearance. Actually, they have been hatching all along, but the water levels are now low and slow enough that an angler can effectively fish them.

Midsummer (June, July, and August)

Much of what happens upstream at this time also happens in this section, but often it happens with much more intensity. There is more of an opportunity to wade, which adds to the illusion because more water can be thoroughly covered. I do believe that some of the hatches of insects here are thicker and a little more predictable.

The caddis is the first major insect to present itself in large numbers. Long riffled areas almost always have caddis hatching out of them. Any of the dry patterns will take fish, as will a variety of emergent pupa patterns. The Sparkle Z-lon Caddis has had its moments for me; it does a good job of imitating an emerger, a cripple, or a caddis stuck in its pupal shuck. This multipurpose fly is very effective, especially when fished from a boat. The Bead Head Caddis Larva Nymph is still extremely effective as a subsurface imitation, as is the Red Fox Squirrel Nymph.

The hatches are usually going full-bore in the late morning. Later in the evening, when the caddis swarm over the riffles to mate and lay their eggs, is another time when fishing can be hot. Diving caddis patterns will provide for some good action on a wet-fly swing through the riffles. This is also a good time for traditional wet flies, soft-hackles, and the Platte River Carey fished in the same manner. The caddis remain fairly consistent throughout the midsummer period, but the hatches get significantly lighter as the season progresses.

I do believe that the *Baetis* species hatches are heavier on this stretch than upstream, although I still haven't experienced a blanket hatch in the summer. The character of much of the water in this stretch makes fishing BWO patterns just a little tougher. When trout are on the BWOs they get fairly finicky, and the presentation has to be just right. Pattern style is also important, and I have done much better with parachute-style drys than with conventionally hackled patterns, although in a pinch I will cut a notch of hackle out of the bottom of the fly so it rides lower on the surface. The no-hackle-style dry fly is effective but very difficult for me to tie, so I reserve the ones I buy for the real tough fish. Very often the fish will become selective to the emerger just under or in the surface film, and a floating nymph pattern can be deadly. When I am wading I usually fish only one of the patterns because a little extra care can be taken presenting the fly to the fish, but when I am floating I like to combine both patterns to cover both stages.

The next major hatch is that of the pale morning dun, and the difference between the upper stretches and this stretch is that the hatches here are thicker and more intense. Most of the traditional nymph, dun, and emerger patterns will take fish during this hatch, but every once in a while the fish get picky. A couple of dun patterns that have taken fish when they seem to be finicky are the Comparadun and René Harrop's Cul de Canard PMD. The characteristic they have in common is a low ride on the surface. Maybe they imitate a cripple or stuck-in-the-shuck individual. They very definitely seem to outfish most other dun patterns at times. The Cul de Canard is fast becoming one of my favorite patterns; it is easy to tie and very effective here and on other waters I have fished. Anglers fishing from a moving boat will appreciate this pattern because it is very easy to see on the water, floats well even in riffly areas, and can readily be manipulated without sinking.

Multiple hatches are very common on this stretch, especially on overcast days. It is not uncommon to see PMDs and BWOs hatching from the same water, or maybe even caddis, so careful observation is needed. Many times the trout will become selective to a single insect and, to make things more complicated, to a single stage of a single insect. Once an angler can identify what that fish is feeding on, he stands a chance at catching it. An angler fishing from a moving boat will have little opportunity to do this, but the wading angler can take all the time he needs to observe a fish. The single fish rising in the shallows during a multiple hatch will be the tough one to take, but fish rising in a riffle or in water where the surface is broken will probably be easier. The good thing about this section of river is that a properly presented fly, no matter what the pattern, will very often be taken. But there are times, however, when the trout become extremely fussy.

There are many other mayfly species that hatch in very limited numbers throughout this section of river. I suspect that there is a minor hatch of western march browns (*Rhithrogena* species) in isolated areas. I have seen these insects on the surface and have witnessed small pods of trout rising to them but have never seen great numbers. The pale evening dun (*Heptagenia* species) is also on the water in limited numbers in the late afternoon and evening. Be aware that these, as well as very limited numbers of other mayflies, are present. If an angler has the time to observe and identify them, the proper pattern can be selected. I don't think the fish become selective to the sparse hatches of these mayflies, but one never knows why a pattern was really refused.

The next major insect to hatch is the Trico (*Tricorythodes* species); it begins around the beginning of August and lasts into September. The morning spinner fall is the important stage to fish; it starts around 9:00 A.M. Most Trico spinner patterns work well, but two seem to do better for me. The Cul de Canard Trico Spinner is usually very effective with the proper presentation, but there are times when I have difficulty seeing it on the surface. The Krystal Flash Winged Trico is a little easier to

Trico time.

see, especially from a distance, and simple to tie. It is also very effective, probably because its visibility makes it easier to fish. These flies can be cast into feeding lanes with more accuracy, and a dragging fly can be detected sooner. This is important when casting to fish in very shallow and clear water with very little current. A dragging fly might spook a trout from its feeding position, which could spook nearby fish.

The spinner fall usually lasts to around noon, or until the wind picks up. The wind plays a significant role on this stretch of water because it can literally blow a hatch off the water. There are certain stretches toward the lower end of this section where the wind blows so hard a floating fisherman has to turn the boat around and row downstream in order to make any headway. At the very least the wind will play havoc with accurate casting. The wading angler might be able to find portions of water that are sheltered from the wind and have some good fishing; the float fisherman will very often have to grin and bear it until shelter is found.

When the hatches are sparse, as on very bright days, or when he's been blown off the water, the angler can always resort to nymph-fishing.

Any general caddis larva, mayfly nymph, and stonefly nymph imitations will take fish here and there. Halfbacks always seem to produce a few fish, as do bead-head-style nymphs. Whether fishing from a boat or wading, an angler can usually do well nymph-fishing this stretch, but in the summer it is simply more fun to fish dry patterns.

Fall (September, October, and November)

The summer has very good hatches of insects, but it also has periods of time when the fishing is poor. The cooler, crisper days of autumn are another matter—they trigger some very good fishing. The trout must sense the coming of hard times and begin to prepare or, more likely, the cooler water temperatures are more to their liking and they feed more readily. After the Labor Day weekend (which happens to be an absolute zoo on this section), the fishing pressure is very light.

There are still Tricos on the water in the morning, but they will soon disappear. Early September has some heavy spinner falls, but they get lighter and lighter as the month wears on. The caddis are still around, but they too begin to fade. The early season has some exceptional fishing in the evenings for diving-caddis patterns fished in the riffles. The lower end of this section is full of riffles, and is the place to be. The daytime hatches get later and later before they fade, and it becomes a matter of being in the right riffle at the right time.

The brown trout are once again becoming selective to the abundant stonefly nymphs, and they are beginning to stack up below some of the riffles prior to spawning. The nymph-fishing is excellent, and the streamer-tossers can get their licks in. Some very large fish can be caught at this time of year and it will pay to fully cover some of the deeper pools and holes with streamer patterns.

Float times are much longer in the autumn because the water is lower and slower. Very often, water that holds fish will have to be floated over because everything else is too shallow to float through. A drift-boat owner may spend a good deal of his time dragging his boat over shallow riffles. The walking fisherman will find the low flows easier to cope with and plenty of water to fish.

I think that the most exciting event on this stretch of water in the fall is the blanket *Baetis* species hatches that sometimes occur. Nasty days that might even see some snow falling but are relatively windless produce some of the best hatches on the river. They even seem easier to fish, because I don't think the fish are as selective as they are to the earlier hatches. Small dry-fly patterns are rarely refused if they are presented properly. Patterns like a small Adams work well, as do the other, more specific, patterns. The hatches start around 11:00 A.M. early in the season and get later and later as the season wears on. I have seen good numbers of duns on the water as late as 5:00 P.M.

The trout seem to prefer the slower sections of water when feeding. Tailouts, sections along steep banks, and long glides all seem to be favorite feeding areas. I have seen entire long glides full of rising fish when hatches are thick. Most of the fish that feed in the center sections of the river are on the smaller side, and the large fish seem to hold as tight to the banks as possible. These hatches will taper off when the weather gets very cold and winter approaches. In some years when it stays mild into November the hatches are still going strong, but they are usually over by late October.

Locally Effective Patterns

Clouser Deep Minnow

Hook:	2-10
Thread:	Black or brown
Eyes:	Lead eyes
Belly:	Light bucktail (olive or yellow), about 20 hairs
Middle:	Krystal Flash (green or orange), about 15 strands
Back:	Dark bucktail (black or brown), about 20 hairs

Parachute Baetis Dun

Hook:	16-22
Thread:	Olive
Tails:	Blue dun hackle fibers, split and divided
Wing:	Blue dun hen hackle tied in a clump as a post for the hackle
Body:	Olive dubbing
Hackle:	Blue dun tied parachute-style

Baetis Floating Nymph

Hook:	16-20
Thread:	Olive or brown
Tails:	Barred bronze wood-duck flank-feather fibers
Rib:	Fine gold or copper wire
Body:	Olive dubbing
Wingcase:	Dark brown, olive, or black closed-cell foam
Legs:	Barred bronze wood-duck flank-feather fibers

Cul de Canard Pale Morning Dun

Hook:	14-18
Thread:	Gray
Tails:	White hackle fibers, split and divided
Body:	Pale yellow or sulphur dubbing
Wing:	White cul de canard feather clump laid back over body
Head:	Pale yellow or sulphur dubbing

Sparkle Z-Lon Caddis

Hook:	12-20
Thread:	Tan or light olive
Shuck:	Amber or dark olive Z-lon fibers
Body:	Tan or light olive Antron
Wing:	Deer hair, tied elk-wing-caddis style

Krystal Flash Winged Trico

Hook:	18-24
Thread:	Black
Tails:	Black hackle fibers
Wings:	Strands of pearlescent Krystal Flash
Body:	Black or dark gray dubbing

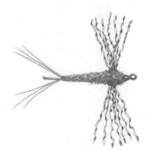

Other Effective Patterns

George's Brown Stone
Cranefly larva
Bitch Creek–Girdle Bug combination
Olive K-Flash Caddis Emerger
Baetis Soft-Hackle
Paratilt
Cul de Canard Trico Spinner
Bead Head Caddis Larva
PMD-Caddis
Platte River Carey
Woolly Buggers
Halfback
Gold-Ribbed Hare's Ear
Red Fox Squirrel Nymph
Herl Nymph
Zug Bug
Prince Nymph
LaFontaine's Emergent Sparkle Pupa
Diving caddis

Adams
March Brown
Pale Evening Dun
Little Blue-Winged Olive
Ginger Quill
Blue Dun
Blue Quill
Royal Trude
Stimulator
Madam X
Kaufmann's Brown Stone
Golden Stone
Yellow Stone Nymph
Montana Nymph
Sparkle Stonefly
Heartwell Stone Nymph
Black Rubberlegs
Brown stimulators
Whitlock Stonefly nymphs

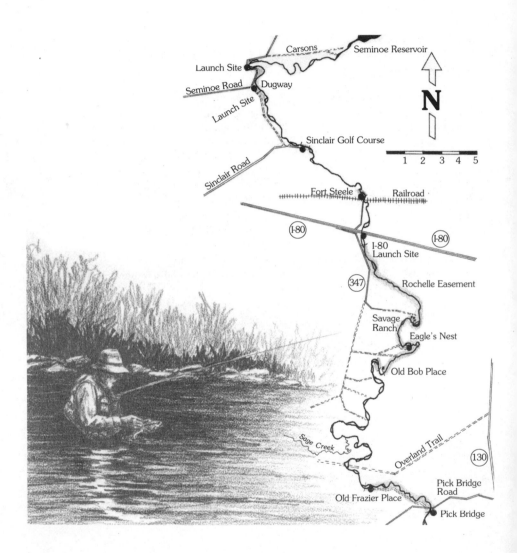

Carsons

Seminoe Reservoir

Launch Site

Seminoe Road Dugway

Launch Site

Sinclair Golf Course

Sinclair Road

N

1 2 3 4 5

Fort Steele Railroad

I-80 I-80

I-80
Launch Site

347 Rochelle Easement

Savage
Ranch Eagle's Nest

Old Bob Place

Sage Creek

Overland Trail 130

Pick Bridge
Road

Old Frazier Place

Pick Bridge

7

Pick Bridge to Seminoe Reservoir

High plains desert is the phrase that best describes this area: the river winds through a mostly treeless, semi-arid, sagebrush-covered, relatively flat terrain. This section begins at the Pick Bridge access area, which has heavy stands of cottonwoods along the river and flows downstream approximately sixty miles until it dumps into Seminoe Reservoir, the first of a series of impoundments that change the character of the river. Long stretches traverse sagebrush country, where the uninitiated would wonder about its ability to hold trout.

Topography

Because long sections of the river carve through wide-open plains, the wind can and usually does make an appearance on a daily basis. The land changes from a transitional marginal bottomland to the sage-shrouded high desert. "Gentle wafting breezes" are not words you'll find in a local's vocabulary here. The wind blows here so often and hard that people would fall on their faces if it should suddenly stop, or so goes the local adage. Usually the wind is tolerable in the morning until noon, when it really picks up. It seems to diminish around dusk. Windless days are not very common along this open stretch of river; the successful fisherman adapts to the various degrees of wind.

A couple other factors must be considered when discussing this stretch. The first is the condition of access roads and launch sites, both of which are poorly maintained at best. In many places, and particularly the Rochelle access, the soil contains bentonite. If it should happen to rain fairly hard, even a four-wheel-drive won't help unless all

115

tires are chained up. This is the slickest, greasiest stuff you can imagine. I strongly urge anyone going in to make a weather check, because it's a long walk out of there.

Another factor to consider concerns the lower reaches of this section, where the river dumps into Seminoe Reservoir. Early spring offers good fishing in this area, but there is a fair amount of alkali in the soil. Keep away from it, particularly if it has just rained—this is nasty stuff.

One more factor needs to be mentioned. This is rattlesnake country, and the wading angler needs to exercise caution. The snakes do come down to the river for water; it is even common to see them swimming the river. Be careful. As isolated as some of these stretches are, a rattler bite could be hours from the nearest treatment.

Water Characteristics

This stretch covers about sixty miles and begins to change from a riffled area at the Pick Bridge access to slower, deeper, siltier sections downstream. There are all kinds of water types here, with the exception of fast rapid-filled areas.

There is a fairly good ratio of riffle, run, and pool areas along the entire stretch, but as one travels downstream the pools begin to turn into long slow glides, and the riffled areas are farther apart. Bottom structure is varied, ranging from gravely rubble to large boulders in the water and along the bank to slow, muddy, silty spots. All kinds of holding water will be found along the way. There are huge backwaters in this area best detected by the rafts of foam covering them. We call them "scum holes," and they are favored spots to fish.

There is some channelization or braiding occurring along the way downstream, but mostly the river is a relatively uniform width. The water depth varies from inches in some of the riffles to double-digit feet in some of the holes. All the various kinds of structure that provide habitat for fish can be found. There are undercut banks, overhanging vegetation, good-sized rocks, downed trees, high banks with pockets cut into them, boulder-lined shores, and even the occasional dead steer—all hold fish. Water speed here is slower than in the upper river because the gradient is not as steep, which probably accounts for the oxbowing that occurs. It is extremely wadable throughout most of the season.

Accessibility

This stretch of river has very good amounts of public access, for Wyoming. Pick Bridge has a good gravel-based road into it that should weather a fairly heavy thunderstorm. At the bridge itself is a camping area with a primitive outhouse and a launch site. (Boat launch sites along the North Platte are merely spaces cut into the bank. There are no gravel or concrete ramps here in Wyoming.) The launches are mostly serviceable but leave a lot to be desired, especially when one gets stuck putting in or taking out his drift boat. The launch at Pick Bridge is slightly better than most because it is relatively level with a good deal of space to maneuver.

There are signs posted that detail the borders of the easement. At the lower end of this access is another small camping area with an outhouse and launch site.

The Pick Bridge access is managed as a trophy fishery, and there is a slot limit in place. Fish between ten and twenty inches must be returned to the water unharmed. Wyoming Fish and Game is also in the process of constructing some instream habitat improvement. Of the entire stretch of river described in this chapter, this area gets the most use and is far and above the most heavily fished. It is close to Saratoga, with a good road and nice scenery. The cottonwood-lined banks and the irrigated fields make it a pleasant place to fish. Holiday weekends should be avoided.

The next major access area is in the vicinity of Rawlins, sixteen miles to the west of the river. The river here flows under I-80 at the Fort Steele rest area. There is a parking area and a take-out site under the interstate bridge. The major access is upstream, south of the interstate. This area is known as the Rochelle easement and runs eleven miles upstream through a good amount of private (the Bolton ranch) land. The road runs along the river for a mile or so and then diverges from it. After the first mile or so, one can reach the river by taking some of the side roads into parking areas, which are poorly marked, if at all. (Signs are not common in this easement.) At the parking areas are outhouses, but no overnight camping is allowed.

I have to admit that, although this is the area I consider my home water, the access is an abomination and the launch sites a nightmare.

Floating at Eagle's Nest.

The launch area at·Eagle's Nest (about the upstream boundary of the easement), approximately ten miles upstream, is very poorly maintained, and in low-water years getting stuck in the sand at the launch is a real possibility. The launch at the Savage ranch site is marginally better, but the last half-mile of the road is a real bear.

The access roads in and out of these individual sites are in poor shape. The main road is in fairly good condition for a gravel-and-dirt road, but not all of it has a gravel bed. Rain could make traveling on this road very tough for even the best four-wheel-drive. A two-wheel-drive will be stuck for quite a while if there should be a heavy rain while the owner is out on the water.

The good news is that an angler could walk the entire eleven miles along the bank if he wanted to. It is especially good here for floaters, who can beach the boat and wade the good-looking water.

The first few miles of the easement get a fair amount of pressure from the local bait and spin fishers. The number of people decreases as one travels upstream, though. This is not a very pressured area. There is no shuttle service available here.

There is also a small access area located just north of the interstate bridge at the old Fort Steele ruins site. Mostly, it's an area where one could launch or take out a boat; there is a very limited area for the wader. As with most of the other launch sites, this is poorly maintained, and there is no real ramp. A level, somewhat rocky opening in the bank is the ramp. It does take quite a bit of maneuvering in tight quarters if you have a trailered boat. Because of vandalism to the area in the past, there is now a locked gate that remains open and unlocked from 7:00 A.M. to 7:00 P.M. Take that into consideration when planning a float.

This access makes a float trip to the Dugway area or the golf course somewhat shorter than from the I-80 bridge. When the wind picks up on one of these floats, an abbreviated trip will seem like a godsend. Also, because the Rochelle easement is so accessible, a variety of float lengths can be customized if one has an easily carried boat, like a canoe or raft, and doesn't mind launching at any spot on the bank. Often, an evening float from the I-80 bridge to the Fort Steele ruins is a pleasant way to get a few hours of fishing into a tight schedule.

Another access area that many of the local folks use is the mile of accessibility along the Sinclair golf course. Many local anglers, mostly bait and spin fishermen, come here to catch a few fish in the morning or evening hours. During the summer it is a popular place to take out a boat, and from the I-80 bridge to the golf course is a popular float. The trouble is that there is no real take-out area. The bank is well above the water line, and getting a boat out of the water is a real chore. There is a chain across the road at the golf course that is locked at night (from around 10:00 P.M. until 7:00 A.M.).

The last major access area is north of the interstate along the road from the town of Sinclair to Seminoe State Park. The area is known as the Dugway, and it has a few miles of access. There is a boat launch and outhouse at the BLM campground and another toward the downstream end of the access. Although there can be some decent fishing there, it is not an area especially used by local fishermen. It is a convenient (but long) take-out for floaters putting in at the interstate bridge.

A few more miles down the river is a local access called Carsons, but I don't believe you'll find it on any map. Many people in the Rawlins-Sinclair area fish here for trout and walleye as the river empties into Seminoe Reservoir. There are no launches or outhouse facilities. Boats are launched and taken out through the low spots along the bank. Roads in and out of the area are so horrible that it's one of those places where you will suggest that a buddy take his vehicle rather than yours. The area does offer some good cutthroat fishing in the fall.

Management

As the river changes on its downstream journey, so does the quality classification. The upstream reach near the Pick Bridge access is still considered Blue Ribbon water, and it is managed as a trophy fishery. The rest of the river to Seminoe is considered Red Ribbon, or second-best.

The Pick Bridge reach has very good holding water and some spawning habitat where Jack Creek empties into the main river. Fish, especially the brown trout, run up it to spawn. If a fly fisher can find access to the creek, some exceptional fishing can be had.

This upstream stretch has more fish per mile than the lower end, and the fish seem to hang around. This doesn't necessarily make the lower stretch a poor fishery—quite the contrary. Some of the best fishing in the entire river can be had there at certain times of the year. The Trico hatch in a normal-water year is awesome.

One reason for the downgraded classification enters the main river about halfway down the stretch: Sage Creek. Sage Creek is a small creek that winds through thirty miles or so of sagebrush-covered terrain rich in bentonite. A moderate rain will wash the bentonite into the main river through Sage Creek. When this happens, the river is ruined. Since bentonite particles are very fine and negatively charged, they do not settle out of the river very readily. In normal- and high-water years it takes a few days to push it all downstream to empty into Seminoe. In low-water years it takes a good ten days before the river is clear enough to be fishable. If an angler plans to fish this area and the river does turn bad, upstream of Sage Creek is usually clear or will clear very quickly.

The ratio of fish species changes as one works his way downstream. There is a good concentration of brown trout in the Pick Bridge area, probably about equal numbers of browns to rainbows with a smattering of cutthroats. In the downstream sections most of the fish will be rainbows, cutthroats make an appearance in good numbers, and the brown

A very good brown. (Photo courtesy Steve Hays)

trout population decreases. These numbers are dependent on Wyoming Fish and Game's stocking programs. Because most of the fish in the upper stretch of this section are wild trout, the species ratio does not change too drastically. Of course, it can be affected by the fish downstream migrating up, but it stays mostly in the same ratios.

The lower reach is affected by what has been stocked and by the time of year. When Seminoe was an excellent brown trout fishery, the lower stretch had many more browns. Since the introduction of walleye (no one is quite sure just how they got into the reservoir system and the river itself) in the 1960s, the brown trout population has steadily decreased.

A side note. The river here is divided into two management areas working out of separate offices in separate towns. The Casper office manages the river from the I-80 bridge to Nebraska, and the Laramie office manages from the I-80 bridge upstream to the Colorado border. I'm afraid this entire stretch is undermanaged. Each management office has other more pressing and interesting concerns to occupy their time.

The Casper area manages several tailwater fisheries along with their associated reservoirs and all the problems of those areas. The Laramie office has ninety miles of free-flowing river, of which at least half is managed as a wild trout fishery with slot limits.

I fear that because the Pick Bridge to Seminoe area (with the exception of the Pick Bridge access itself) does not get the numbers of fishermen demanding more fish, bigger fish, and better facilities, all the efforts of Wyoming Fish and Game go into the more prestigious and visible sections of the river. It's a catch-22: When asked why the area isn't better managed, both offices state that it isn't fished enough to warrant improvement, but the reason it isn't fished as much as other sections is because of the poor accessibility and smaller numbers of fish.

Throughout the years, the department of fish and game has experimented with different stocking programs, and several interesting things have developed. When the walleye population increased, the trout stocking program had a very limited success. By trial and error the department realized that in order for most of the stocked trout to survive they should be a little larger than half of the length of the average walleye; otherwise, the walleye would feed on them.

Many hatchery-reared rainbows are traditionally lake-oriented fish, so different strains of rainbows would leave the river to make their way to Seminoe, decreasing the population in the river. The Eagle Lake rainbows, on the other hand, enter the river on spawning runs, thereby increasing the population in the river at various times of the year, even though they return to the reservoir.

There are also two different strains of cutthroats in the river: the Yellowstone and the Snake River. At one time, fish and game was aggressively stocking cutthroats in the lower reach of this section. They were "catchables" of eight to twelve inches, stocked primarily for many of the local bait and spin fishermen who tended to keep limits of fish.

Wyoming Fish and Game stated it believes a full two-thirds of the fish in the lower section of the river have been stocked in or near Seminoe Reservoir and have migrated upstream. Springtime sees a large concentration of rainbows and cutthroats as they enter the river seeking spawning areas. Fall sees the brown trout enter for the same reasons, but not in the numbers of the past, when Seminoe was an excellent brown fishery.

Because Seminoe is so near, the fish in the lower section of the river will often move back into the reservoir when water conditions in the river deteriorate. Very-low-water years will move fish to the reservoir, especially when they are combined with high water temperatures and extended periods of siltation. The cold of late fall and early winter will cause the fish to move back. A low-water year with relatively high water temperatures makes fishing in this area very chancy—some other section of the river will be a better bet.

Seasonal Changes in Fishing

This portion of the river remains free-flowing and unblocked by any impoundment until it reaches Seminoe Reservoir, thus it is highly susceptible to climatic changes during the prime of the season and the year in general. Water taken for irrigation affects the river to a lesser degree. As the year develops, many things happen to the river that affect and determine its fishability.

Here is a case of a river deciding when, where, and how an angler can pursue his sport. Winter means an ice-choked river with virtually no fishing available to the fly fisher. As spring approaches and the ice breaks up, the fishing opportunities begin to pick up. Some surprisingly good fishing can be had during the period between ice-out and the beginning of runoff.

Spring (March, April, and May)

Somewhere around the middle of March is a seven- to ten-day period when the ice has broken up and the surges of runoff haven't taken full effect. This period does not occur every year and the timing can be too chancy to plan a special trip here, but if one happens to be in the area anyway, the fishing can be very good.

At this time, many of the rainbows that have migrated back into Seminoe Reservoir for the winter and a good deal of reservoir resident rainbows move into the river with hopes of spawning. The cutthroats tend to move into the river later in the spring, usually when runoff is in full swing. The water conditions are generally low and clear (clear enough to fish), giving the fisherman a window of opportunity before the turmoil of runoff sends him looking for still water or some tailwater. Both air and water temperatures are on the cool side, so dress accordingly.

Most of the fishing will be with nymphs or streamers. No matter how you fish, your offering should be presented on or near the stream bottom. Food sources come alive at this time of year—not that they were dormant all winter long, but they do seem to be plentiful. The caddis larvae have grown to an almost mature state in anticipation of pupating and emerging during the late spring or early summer. There are predominantly *Hydropsyche* and *Brachycentrus* larvae in the river. I'm sure there are many other kinds of caddisflies present, but these two seem to be the dominant genera in this section of river. Any acceptable caddis larva or cased caddis pattern will catch fish. Long-nosed dace are abundant in the riffles, so the appropriate streamer pattern should produce. Many mayfly nymphs will have grown to a size that trout will readily ingest.

In my opinion, the most important insect on the bottom of the river is a medium-sized stonefly nymph of the Perlidae family. It is some sort of golden stone species, possibly a brown willow fly. The bottom of the river is literally covered with these nymphs along most of this stretch. The adults never become important because they seem to emerge at the height of the runoff. Although there is a steady emergence into October, the numbers aren't enough to attract the fish. These nymphs have grown through their many instars to reach full size, from one to one and a half inches long, prior to emerging. They live in the riffles and fast-water areas of the stream, but they move to slower areas to emerge. This migration of the mature nymphs makes them available to the trout. They are plentiful and the rainbows feed heavily on them, as autopsies on many fish attest. Any medium-sized (about #8) Golden Stonefly nymph pattern worked near the bottom will attract fish.

These stonefly nymph imitations should be the fly fisher's main weapon during this brief period, for obvious reasons. Since these stoneflies are present in the river all year long, they require two to three years to fully develop. So, smaller-sized patterns should be a part of any angler's fly box. They can be fished all during the season with good success. A Halfback will often succeed when all else fails.

Fishing appears to be better in the lower reach of this section with the stonefly type patterns, especially in the Carsons and Dugway areas because the majority of migrating fish hit these areas first. By the time the fish work their way into the Rochelle easement, runoff usually has begun. The upper reach near Pick Bridge seems to have more caddis larvae than stoneflies, although both insects are there in profusion. Experiment with various patterns to find the fly *du jour*.

A plus at this time of year is that one can sleep in and still get into the good fishing. Usually late morning to midafternoon is the best time to fish. The water is cold at this time of year, and any rise in temperature will trigger some feeding activity on the trout's part. When the temperature starts to drop in the late afternoon, so does the quality of the fishing.

Although this runoff period is shortlived, it is worthwhile fishing. Many of the fish caught at this time of year will be somewhat emaciated due to the marginal food supplies of the winter. Treat them gently so they may continue to offer sport when they do fatten up.

Runoff means a fly fisher heads for lakes, ponds, reservoirs, tail-waters, and other parts of the country. In normal-water years, runoff could start in mid-March and last until mid-June. High-water years will see runoff conditions into July. Very-low-water years could find it completed by Memorial Day weekend. There are hatches that do occur during the runoff period, but they usually cannot be fished.

Early Summer (End of May to the Beginning of July)

As runoff begins to abate, water conditions begin to clear. This signals the start of the fishing season. Twelve to eighteen inches of visibility is the barometer by which one can measure the fishability of the river. This happens in early June, but if I had to pinpoint a date, I'd say the tenth of June could be it.

With eighteen inches of visibility and high water comes the floating season. A drift fisherman can cover fairly long distances and throw streamers and large nymphs against the banks. This technique is the same as practiced on the upper river. Large attractor-type dry flies may be fished by the floater. Generally, the water at the stream's edge is clearer than is the current flow itself. Fish holding along the bank in this quieter water will often take the dry. Rainbows, cutthroats, and browns will be available at this time, with an occasional walleye showing up for bottom-draggers.

The wading fisherman will have success, but his fishing may be limited due to the higher, faster flows. With all the access available here, the wader can catch his share of fish. One problem he may encounter is

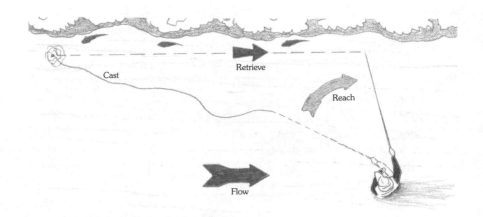

Presenting a Streamer Upstream

1. Cast.
2. Reach to bank so path of fly is presented to fish along the bank.
3. Retrieve *just* fast enough to match current speed.

that the stronger flows tend to push the fish to the banks. Unless a wader can work his streamer along the banks, his success will be limited. A good technique for the wader is to cast upstream along the bank, if possible, and retrieve just fast enough to control the line but slow enough to make the artificial appear as if it were trapped in the current. An occasional twitch creates enough of a struggling-baitfish effect to trigger strikes. Remember that the current is fast and the fish do need a little time to decide whether to strike or refuse. A fast downstream stripping action will result in few fish. Casting out and downstream is not as effective because the presentation borders on an unnatural action at this time; a baitfish will find it difficult to swim up against these strong flows. Working a wadable section of water with a large nymph is very productive at this time.

As the season moves on in a few weeks and the water temperature begins to warm and the flows drop, the river is in its prime. The insect activity begins in full force and the fishing can be at its best. This usually happens toward the end of June. So much happens on the river now that it becomes a feast for the fish. Caddis begin their emergence in huge

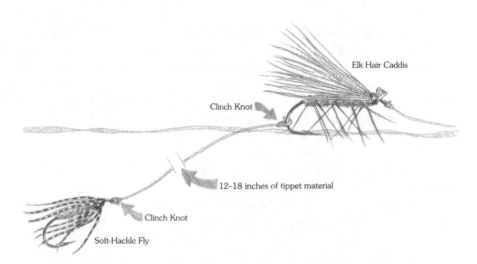

Elk Hair Caddis

Clinch Knot

12–18 inches of tippet material

Clinch Knot

Soft-Hackle Fly

An Elk Hair Caddis–to–Soft-Hackle Setup

numbers, offering some wonderfully easy fishing. Any riffled section of river should see good caddis activity in the late morning hours, although the angler should be prepared for a caddis emergence at any time of day—morning, midday, late afternoon, or late evening. There are times when caddis appear to emerge all day long.

The caddis emergence is fun to fish because it is often very easy to fish. If you are a beginning angler, fishing the emergence could give you the confidence to continue fly fishing. A good way to fish the emergence is with a soft-hackled fly or an emerger pattern (like LaFontaine's Emergers), using the wet-fly swing through the riffles. I like fishing two flies at this time. I use an Elk Hair Caddis pattern as a dropper about a foot or so above a soft-hackled point fly (see illustration above). This way, I can fish the Elk Hair as an adult caddis with a drag-free float; then, as it begins to drag on its down-and-across-current path, the soft-hackle comes into play, imitating an emerging caddis.

Often the soft-hackle will be taken during the drag-free drift, or the Elk Hair will be taken as it drags across the surface. Cutthroats are notorious for taking a fly presented in this manner. (This is a fun method to use to teach a child fly-fishing skills, because accurate casts are not critical to success.)

Mayfly activity begins in strength at this time. This stretch of river has a wide variety of mayfly species—some become extremely important to the angler, others only marginally important, and a few not important at all. Green and gray drakes are in this section of river, but I have never seen them hatch in numbers sufficient to be classified as a hatch. The same goes for a variety of mayflies that may be found in other sections of this stretch.

The first of the mayfly species that makes an appearance belongs to the *Baetis* genus. There are at least two major hatches during the season: one in the early summer and one in the fall. The end of June and the beginning of July see little blue-winged olives and another may-fly with a grayish tan body make their debuts. They come during the wild time of the caddis emergence and appear to hatch at around the same time of day. They are often overshadowed by the flashiness of the caddis, and many anglers simply overlook fish rising to these other small insects.

The floating angler may run across pockets of fish that are highly selective to the tinier *Baetis* species. A few of the favorite places to run into fish feeding on *Baetis* duns are the quieter waters along the sides of riffles or in the eddies or backwaters, where the fish can leisurely sip the duns off the surface. Often a fly fisher will see the slashing rises to caddis while the sipping takes go unnoticed. Putting a caddis imitation over a fish that is keyed to the smaller *Baetis* species will usually lead to a frustrating day. Once the angler realizes that a multiple hatch is taking place, he can then effectively take fish. A #18 dry will usually take fish, and a specific *Baetis* pattern like a No-Hackle, Comparadun, or Blue-Winged Olive will definitely take fish. If no specific pattern is available in your fly box, a small Adams will do.

These are not heavily fished trout, and as long as the presentation is good the specific pattern is not too important. However, if the fish are working a stretch of smooth clear water, a surface-film-emerger pattern can be the ticket to good action. A split-tailed, sparsely hackled

pattern with a dubbed body and a foam ball on top is a good bet under
these conditions. The foam ball enables the pattern to lie flush in the
surface film. Drop one of these imitations into the feeding lane of a fish
and it will seldom be refused.

Around this time of year a mayfly that I would consider marginally
important to the fly fisher makes an appearance and should be discussed.
I have always noticed a mayfly dun on the water that fish never seemed
to take, for whatever reason. These little yellow mayfly (*Epeorus* species)
duns would drift undisturbed down the currents, and I figured that the
trout did not like them. Then, one low-water year, the river dropped
and cleared earlier than usual. I was fishing the Rochelle easement when
the yellow duns started to pop onto the surface in some—not overwhelming—numbers, but enough to apparently interest the fish. This
was in the late afternoon. Of course, I didn't have any pattern to match
this hatch because the flies have a distinctive yellow body and wings.
They are fairly large, about #10 or #12. I used a large light Cahill that
I managed to find in my vest and caught some fish. I went home and
tied up a handful of #12 yellow mayflies, figuring I would have these
forever because I must have witnessed a fluke event. I returned to the
river the next afternoon and, much to my surprise, the same thing happened. This time I was prepared and did well on the fish. Some of the
brown trout I caught measured twenty-one inches. This hatch continued
for about a week before it petered out.

This mayfly hatches throughout the season and never again does
it seem to become important to the fish. I can often watch these yellow
duns drift on the surface until they are totally out of sight, and no fish
take them. I can only surmise that in low-water years they must hatch
in enough volume to make them important to fish. In high-water years
the hatch either goes unnoticed on my part or on the fishes'. I suspect
that I'm not paying attention. In any case, if it is a low-water year and
early June, carry a few yellow duns just to be sure.

In some of the slower sections of the river, midges are always present
for the morning fisherman. I don't know too many people who consider them important enough to be worth fishing. All the problems associated with midging make the casual angler unwilling to tackle these
fish, because midges seem to make even the most unsophisticated fish
ultraselective.

Midsummer (July and August)

As we enter the month of July, one of the premier hatches begins to take shape: that of the pale morning dun (*Ephemerella* species). The nymphs are an important food source in the entire river system. A PMD pattern I use probably accounts for over eighty percent of the fish I catch in a given year. One year I kept accurate records of where, when, how, and with what I fished: the PMD nymph outfished everything else I used.

A good day for PMDs to hatch is any summer day that is overcast and drizzly. If you should be in the area when this type of weather is evident, beat it to the water because you'll have fishing you won't believe. On clear, warm days the hatches are sporadic.

By this time the trout have been conditioned to surface activity, so there are almost always surface-feeding fish somewhere along this stretch of river. The pale morning dun hatches out in the riffle sections, but the trout mostly feed on them in the slower water of the pools and glides downstream. Look in the edges of the quieter water along the riffles for a few fish feeding; they are often hard to detect, and some are quite large.

This is a good time of year to make short floats of about three miles. Good water can be worked from outside the boat, and enough water can be covered to find the surface-feeding pods of fish. It should be noted that the fish in this stretch of river seem to feed in pods. A wading fisherman may constantly fish an area where there are no surface-feeding fish and may wonder about the quality of the fishing when, at the same time up or down the river, other fishermen are having the time of their lives fishing to rising fish.

Short floats are recommended because the water speed is slower than upstream, and if feeding fish are discovered and sufficiently worked, it may be a very late and dark journey down the rest of the river. Short floats will enable you to enjoy the hatch without tempting your judgment.

The PMD hatch starts at about 10:00 or 11:00 A.M. and lasts until about 2:00 P.M. or whenever the wind pushes you off the water. Many fish will be found in the currents toward the center of the river, but watch the banks for those lazy fish not willing to work for their food. I like to fish with a nymph in the morning until I see duns coming off the water. An emerger or stuck-in-the-shuck pattern will continue to take fish. When a good number of duns start appearing, the fish seem to selectively key on them, so I switch to an adult pattern and move downstream to the pools and glides to continue fishing. In the evening, when the hatch is completely over, there is a spinner fall that I occasionally like to fish. The quieter water along the banks is good water to work with a Rusty Spinner pattern.

A mayfly that is not too important on this river but that makes an appearance at this time is the pale evening dun. It provides for some limited dry-fly action in the late afternoon and evening. If the weather is on the cool and wet side, the hatching duns will usually stay on the water for a few feet of drift. In clear warm weather these mayflies seem to pop off the surface and fly away immediately after emerging, giving the trout very little opportunity to feed on them. Often, what looks like a trout surface-feeding is actually a trout feeding on an emergent pale evening dun as it quickly buoys to the surface. An emergent pattern fished on a wet-fly swing or with a Leisenring Lift will produce fish. This can be a tough hatch to fish because the trout will key on the nymph that is rapidly rising to the surface and not the duns, which don't seem to stay on the surface very long

Yellow sallies also make their debut about this time. This little yellow stonefly resembles a caddisfly, and an Elk Hair Caddis is a good imitation of it. They emerge in the afternoon by crawling out of the water onto sticks or rocks. There is a movement of nymphs to the slower sections of the stream prior to emergence. A Hare's Ear fished with a slow retrieve will imitate this action nicely. In the evenings the adult yellow sallies come to the faster water of the riffles in swarms to lay their eggs by dipping their abdomens into the water. This activity does interest the trout, as demonstrated by the splashy show-off riseforms they make feeding on these stoneflies. There will be days in July when you'd swear nothing was happening on the river. Maybe the wind has been blowing so hard that the fish have been put off the hatches, or maybe the fish are on vacation. There are still a number of things the angler can do to catch fish. One is to nymph-fish, using a PMD nymph coupled with a #8 Halfback. This combination can be deadly on this stretch of river. Dead-drift this setup along the bottom and let the Halfback (as point fly) swing across the current at the end of the drift. I think more fish have been caught on a Halfback swinging across the current on this section of river than on all other patterns combined.

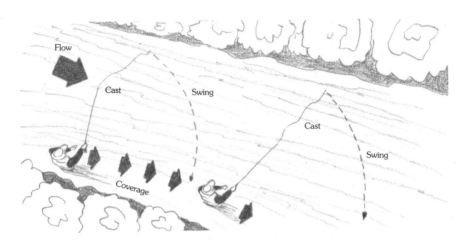

The Wet Fly Swing

1. Start at head of riffle. Cast across and let fly swing in the current.
2. Take one step downstream and repeat.
3. Move to end of riffle, where current evens out.
4. Make sure cast is to *fast* water and the swing is into *slower* water.

Another technique that is very effective is to use a Platte River Carey with a wet-fly swing through the riffles and runs (see illustration above). Cutthroats, browns, and rainbows have all been taken with this technique, but it's especially deadly on the cutthroats. The key is to cast to faster water and swing into the slower water.

This is the time of year when the river becomes extremely susceptible to the whims of nature. Rains can roil the water and put off fishing opportunities for a few days. High temperatures can heat the river and make fishing a frustrating search for anything that resembles a strike. Very low water, feeble flows, and then a sudden flood could send a surge of bentonite silt into the river, making clearing seem like a forever experience.

August is Trico time, and *Tricorythodes* species appear in astonishing numbers. Walking along the upper Rochelle shoreline in the morning hours anytime after the first week in August, one can see spectrelike clouds waving in the light breeze. What appears to be smoke wafting up into the sky is actually swarms of mating Tricos, millions of insects. It is a spectacular sight.

A Trico mating swarm.

Trim off bottom hackle

Rides low on the surface

A Clipped Platte River Adams

Tricos are interesting little bugs. Apparently the males of the species
hatch at night starting about eleven o'clock, while the females hatch
in the predawn darkness to a little after first light. To effectively fish the
hatch, one should hit the water very early in the morning. The Tricos
go through their mating rituals in huge swarms. Sometime around
9:00 A.M. the spinners fall and the real fishing begins.

Trico duns are very tiny, and an accurate representation should be
tied on #24, #26, or #28 hooks. But thanks to the fishing gods, such
isn't necessary on this stretch of river. I usually fish #16, #18, and #20
patterns. I particularly favor a #18 or #20 Platte River Adams with the
hackle trimmed from the bottom (see illustration above). It takes its share
of fish and, more importantly, I can usually see it on the water.

The fish are not pattern- or size-selective, but that does not mean
they are stupidly easy to catch. They are ultraselective to one thing,
and that is presentation. A poorly presented fly will go unnoticed at
best or will put down the fish at worst. During the Trico spinner fall,
so many insects end up on the water that the fish move to the very
shallow water of the slow slicks. There may be some fish rising out in
the current, but my experience has shown these fish to be on the smallish
side. The larger fish move to the banks, often in water so shallow their

dorsal fins are visible. Here they rhythmically sip spent Tricos off the surface. Very little energy is wasted getting food because a fish will rarely move three inches to either side.

A drag-free float is imperative because the insects are dead and motionless. Any pattern that drags in front of a fish will appear to be alive and thus refused because of its unnatural appearance.

A drag-free float must occur exactly in the feeding lane of a particular fish. Often, a fisherman will try for a single fish, and because of an inability to make a proper cast or an intervening current will become frustrated and start changing flies or move on to a different fish. Often, all that is needed to hook these fish is a minor change in position — either up, down, or closer to the fish. Before changing flies or trying another fish during the spinner-fall, assume that your fly is dragging and make the necessary adjustments.

These fish are remarkably easy to approach from midstream. The bank feeders are extremely wary of predators because they are exposed in the shallow, slow, clear water. If the angler tries to approach them from the bank side, the fish will bolt to the safety of deeper water, and some will stay down for the day. Apparently, these fish look to the bank for danger from approaching predators and the midstream corridor represents safety. An angler approaching from midstream can carefully wade very close to feeding fish without putting them down. Of course, wading-induced waves or sloppy casts will put the fish down anyway, but usually they will return to their feeding lanes after a few minutes of quiet. I cannot overemphasize the necessity of getting into the water and fishing toward the bank.

Early August will often have overlapping hatches. It is not uncommon to start fishing the Trico spinner fall and then switch to a PMD hatch; the Trico spinners stop falling around noon, when the PMD hatch is well on its way. An overcast day in early August can provide some awesome fishing.

As August pushes on, the Trico hatch intensifies and peaks around the middle of the month. Although this hatch occurs along the entire stretch of river, the upper Rochelle easement has the most intense action, even though the angler may not see fish rising everywhere in the river. The fish feed in pods, so the angler must find the pods before fishing. Short floats can do this really well even though the water is low and slow.

I recommend short floats because once a pod is located it would be awful to leave it because of the necessity to make up time.

Scum-hole fishing becomes an interesting diversion for anglers along this stretch of river. The backwaters usually are covered with a layer of brownish foam, often two inches thick. These backwaters become places where spent insects are captured by the foam, much to the delight of the fish. These "holes" usually have some depth, and many trout will lie under the foam, feeding on the spent insects. An angler can ascertain where fish are feeding by the subtle bulges in the foam. A fly cast into this mess and ever so slowly retrieved will take some surprisingly large fish.

Late August usually brings low, clear flows to the river, and the cool nights signal some changing weather approaching. The Tricos are generally still available, the PMDs have waned, and most of the other assorted mayfly species have finished. Midday fishing can be spotty at best as the end of the season approaches. But evening can provide some really interesting fishing because a couple of things happen. The egg-laying caddis return to the riffles to lay eggs either by dipping onto the surface or by actually diving down into the water, swimming to the bottom to lay their eggs, and returning to the surface. Many caddis return to the very same riffle they emerged from. All this activity seems to get the attention of the trout. The Pick Bridge access area has become a favorite spot in which to use LaFontaine's Diving Caddis with a wet-fly swing for some super evening fishing. Start at the head of a riffle, cast across, let the fly swing, and do nothing. Strikes can occur anywhere along the swing and anywhere in the riffle. I try to work down into a pool where the current slows too much for the swing to be effective. This has kept me occupied on many evenings until after dark, much to the annoyance of my wife.

Fall (September, October, and November)
As August turns into September, most of the major hatches have ended and the weather turns cooler, decidedly so on particular days. The Tricos are on the wane, but the dry-fly fishing is not over. At this time the *Baetis* start another emergence period and the hatch will last through October into November if the weather allows. An interesting observance about this hatch is that as the water and air temperatures

cool the hatch occurs later and later in the day. In early September, *Baetis* duns will be on the water by 11:00 A.M., but as the cooler weather hits it's often midafternoon before the hatch is in full swing. Overcast days produce the better hatches. On a trip in early October one year, a steady snow fell as we floated the river. It was cold, but it did bring one of the best *Baetis* hatches I have ever seen and some spectacular fishing.

September also brings a rather bizarre hatch: the *Ephoron* species, locally called white miller. The *Ephoron* duns are huge white mayflies (about #10) that have some peculiar traits. They hatch at dusk into total darkness and the spinner fall occurs at the same time the duns emerge. It's a literal blizzard on a warm September evening. As the hatch gets into full swing, there are so many insects coming off the surface, swarming, and falling back to the surface that it appears to be snowing in the twilight. I like to fish an extended-body dun with white hackle tied parachute-style or with the bottoms clipped out of conventionally wound patterns. I believe that the lower profile could adequately represent both the dun and the spentwing.

This hatch is confined to the lower reach of this section of river. I have seen it at the I-80 bridge but not much farther upstream. The Dugway area has the most prolific hatch of these flies. It can happen as early as late August, but the second week of September, depending on weather and water conditions, is usually the peak period. It usually runs strong for about three weeks.

There is some super fishing yet to be had as fall progresses: the *Baetis* hatch is still on, there are some late caddis hatches, and streamer fishing picks up. By being in the right riffle at the right time a fisherman can have a very pleasant day fishing a late caddis emergence. On the other hand, it could be really miserable on a cold, blustery day.

Floating at this time of year can open up some of the better fishing opportunities. A floater can throw streamers in the morning hours, fish the *Baetis* hatch in the midday, and even get into some late-afternoon caddis action. Streamer fishing is usually a pretty good bet in the fall. The fish are probably not so conditioned to the hatches and are always looking for food that can help them prepare for the lean winter months ahead. Many of the brown trout are beginning their spawning activities and become a little more aggressive and territorial, and streamers often

simply tick them off so that they
strike. One thing I have noticed is
that there is a profusion of short
strikes on streamers on the colder
mornings of the fall. The addition
of a stinger hook can solve some
of that problem.

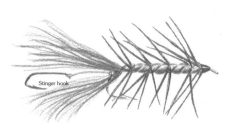

The Pick to Seminoe area may
not have the most fish of the system, the biggest fish, nor the most
beautiful vistas, but it does provide
the angler with some unique fishing opportunities. As the area continues in its trophy management

**Woolly Bugger
with Stinger Hook**

plan, more and better fish will be caught and discussed.

Locally Effective Patterns

Platte River Adams

Hook: 14-22
Thread: Gray, black, or brown
Tail: Grizzly hackles
Body: Gray poly or muskrat
            dubbing
Wing: Single tuft of white poly
            yarn
Hackle: Grizzly and brown mixed

Scum Bug

Hook: 14-20
Thread: Black
Tail: Moose body hair
Body: Black poly dubbing
Wing: Tuft of white poly yarn or
            fluorescent red-orange yarn
Hackle: Golden badger

Cased Caddis Larva

Hook:	10-14
Thread:	Olive or brown
Case:	Pheasant rump feathers palmered on hook then trimmed to shape of case
Body:	Cream or pale yellow dubbing
Legs:	Pheasant-rump-feather fibers

Diving Caddis

Hook:	10-16
Body:	Light brown sparkle yarn
Underwing:	Dark partridge fibers
Overwing:	Clear Antron fibers or white Z-lon
Hackle:	Brown

Little Yellow Mayfly

Hook:	10-16
Thread:	Yellow
Tails:	Yellow hackle fibers, split and divided
Body:	Yellow poly dubbing
Wing:	Single tuft of yellow poly yarn
Hackle:	Yellow

White Miller

Size: 10-14
Thread: White
Tails: White deer hair
Ribbing: Pearl Flashabou
Body: White poly dubbing over
            monofilament extension
Wing: White deer hair butts tied
            as a single clump and
            trimmed into wing
Hackle: White, tied parachute-style

Golden Stone Nymph

Hook: 4-10
Thread: Brown
Tails: Two amber goose biots
Ribbing: Light T.P. amber
            Swannundaze
Abdomen: Hare's ear and golden stone
            dubbing mixed fifty-fifty
Wingcase: Brown mottled turkey quill
            section
Thorax: Same as abdomen
Hackle: Grizzly and brown mixed
            and clipped on bottom
Antennae: Two amber goose biots

PMD Nymph

Hook: 14-18
Thread: Brown
Tails: Barred mallard-flank-
            feather fibers
Ribbing: Copper wire
Abdomen: Light olive, golden stone,
            and hare's ear dubbing,
            blended
Wingcase: Barred mallard flank
            feather pulled over thorax
Thorax: Same as abdomen
Legs: Fibers from wingcase tied
            back

Other Effective Patterns

Adams
Light Cahill
Gold-Ribbed Hare's Ear
Halfback
Woolly Buggers (olive, black)
Pheasant Tail Nymph
Baetis Soft-Hackle
Baetis Emerging Nymph
Blue-Winged Olive
Blue Dun
Pale Morning Emerging Dun
Pale Morning Comparadun

Rusty Spinner
Trico Spinner
Partridge and Yellow Soft-Hackle
Little Yellow Stone
Bucktail caddis
Elk Hair Caddis
Zug Bug
Platte River Carey
Herl Nymph
Prince Nymph
Bead Head Caddis Larva
Red Fox Squirrel Nymph

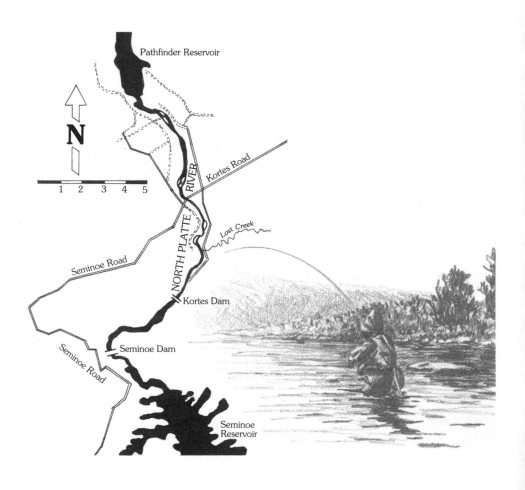

Pathfinder Reservoir

Kortes Road

NORTH PLATTE RIVER

Lost Creek

Seminoe Road

Kortes Dam

Seminoe Dam

Seminoe Road

Seminoe Reservoir

N

1 2 3 4 5

8

The Miracle Mile

The Miracle Mile of the North Platte River is a section that connects two reservoirs: Kortes and Pathfinder. In normal water years it is about seven miles in length, but recent low-water years have extended it to about fifteen miles (this is because of the unusual drawdown of Pathfinder Reservoir). It is the first of a series of tailwater fisheries as the river flows downstream.

When I first moved into the area the obvious question on my mind was: Why the name? The stories of the great numbers and sizes of the fish usually caught here soon convinced me that the name was appropriate. I began grilling anyone I could find who fished the Mile about just how they fished. To a person, I was told that the only way to be successful was to fish with streamers, particularly the Platte River Special variations. I learned of the huge assortment of variations, and everyone seemed to have their own pet pattern. Armed with this knowledge, a box full of streamers, and an eagerness (mind you, eagerness is very much an understatement) to get out and catch a few, I headed for the Mile. I fished these streamers upstream, downstream, quartering up, quartering down, and every other way I could think of, with very little success. Okay, I thought, the fish must not be in a feeding mode. I'll come back another day. I came back and back and back until I began believing that the reason this section is called the Miracle Mile is because it's a miracle if a fish is ever caught here.

I finally did come to my senses and realized that flogging away with streamers was not necessarily the way to fish. After all, this is a tailwater and should be fished like a tailwater. I was overcome by the lore of local knowledge, a newness to the West, and visions of huge fish, easily caught. Only when I buckled down and got to sensibly fishing the way I knew how did I start having success. Now, based on experience, I can honestly and enthusiastically state that the Miracle Mile is truly a wondrous fishery.

It is, in my opinion, the best trophy-trout fishery in the state of Wyoming (moving water fishery, that is; there are some public and private still waters that hold some extraordinarily large fish). Apparently, I am not the only fisherman who thinks this; this piece of water is probably the most-fished stretch in the state. Hardly a day goes by when there isn't someone fishing the Mile, even in some of the nastiest winter weather. There are certain times of the year when finding a decent spot to fish on the Mile is tough because of the crowds.

But this is a trophy fishery in every sense of the word. I have caught trout over ten pounds in this wonderful stretch of water. It is my firm belief that an average fisherman will at least hook a trophy fish (five pounds and larger) nearly every day he fishes here at certain times of the year, and will have the opportunity to hook one any time of the year. I don't know too many other fisheries where this can happen.

Topography

This unique stretch of river begins at the outflow of Kortes Reservoir in a rather steep canyon and winds its way downstream to a high-desert landscape. On the east side of the river are the Seminoe mountains forming an interesting backdrop, and on the west side of the river is the high-desert land with sage-covered hills. The river flows into Pathfinder Reservoir and, depending on the volume of water in the reservoir, the river can flow through a flat area that is normally the reservoir bed when full. Along the east bank in this lower end are some high banks and chalk cliffs; the west bank becomes a plain.

There is some conifer foliage along the east bank in the canyon area of the river. As one progresses downstream, the banks have some willows and an occasional cottonwood or stand of cottonwoods. Along some areas of the river is a sage-covered bank. Mostly the banks have sparse foliage, so the wading fisherman can cast without too much concern for his backcast. The banks themselves vary in height from rather steep drops to gradually sloped, grassy areas. This is an easy stretch of river to bank-fish from.

Seminoe Dam and Kortes Reservoir. (Photo courtesy Steve Hays)

Water Characteristics

The Miracle Mile is a tailwater, therefore the water is governed by what happens at the dam. If a great deal of water is let out, then the downstream section of river can be a torrent; on the other hand, if the outflow is scant, the downstream sections can become a trickle. This is not a tailwater that has any set schedule for the release of water—it occurs randomly. A local adage for describing the water flows says to place a twenty-dollar bill on a nearby rock when wading, and when it begins to float away start heading for the shore. I don't know where this comes from because most of my friends regard a twenty-dollar bill as a week's wages. But I think if enough out-of-state fishermen abide by this, my friends will be waiting downstream with dip nets.

The amount of water released from the dam is determined by the irrigation needs of the water-right holders downstream. Water rights in the West is a complicated issue. I cannot even pretend to understand all the politics and legalities involved; all I know is how they affect the fishing on the Mile.

Water may be released at any time of day and in any volume based on the downstream call. There is no warning siren, as some rivers below dams have, and there seems to be no set schedule. The river usually does not rise fast, so one can usually exit the stream safely. I remember fishing a river Back East where anglers had five minutes to exit the stream after the siren went off or else be swept along a three-foot surge. Although there is no surge on the Mile, there have been times when I was concentrating on the fishing and didn't pay any attention to the slowly rising water, which made my return to shore rather wet. A few drownings over the years here can probably be, at least in part, attributed to the water rising and catching anglers unaware.

Obviously, the spring and summer months have the greatest fluctuations because these are the prime irrigation months. The winter months can bring fairly constant flows or varied flows depending on which reservoir is being dewatered to make room for runoff. If Seminoe is being filled as a storage container, then the Mile will have very little change in flow, and that will be minimal. There is a minimum-flow regulation of 500 cfs in effect. If Seminoe is being dewatered to fill a downstream reservoir, then the Mile will have heavy flows that are very tough to fish. When Seminoe is dewatered in the winter months, the ice fishermen are often very surprised after drilling a hole and looking at the water level some twelve feet below them. Many of them fall spreadeagle in a heartbeat—can you imagine falling through the ice into water some dozen feet or so below the ice? In one very high water year, Seminoe was being emptied so fast that the water in the Mile was out of its banks for an extended period. The fish moved out of the river itself into areas of slower water that are normally above the high-water mark to escape the heavy flows. This made for some very peculiar fishing—fish were caught beneath picnic tables, among other unlikely spots.

The water-level fluctuations do affect the fishing, at times dramatically. If the water is on the rise, wading may be a bit more difficult, but the fishing usually remains fairly good. But if the water begins to fall, then the fish seem to move to the deeper channels in the stream as a protective reflex and become difficult to catch. A constant flow over an extended period of time, usually a few days, makes for the best fishing conditions. The fish will stay in certain areas, so the angler will have a chance to fish for them. The fluctuating water constantly moves fish around, so locating groups of fish may be tricky. The angler who doesn't understand this will hammer fish in a spot one day and wonder what he is doing wrong the next when the fishing is very poor. He may be doing nothing wrong other than fishing an area that has been vacated by the fish due to water-level changes. Even if the flows are very high, if they remain constant for a few days, fish can be caught.

The nature of the water during average flows is like most other sections of the river upstream. There is fast white water in some of the steeper gradients, and slow, deep pools. There is a very good ratio of riffles to runs and pools, with all kinds of water types in between. Some of the faster water can be difficult and, at times, almost impossible to wade. There is a good amount of braiding and channeling because of the numerous small islands along most of the Mile. There is a water type somewhere here that will suit the needs of any kind of angler.

The bottom of the river ranges from large boulders to a silty muck, but the dominant feature is mostly largish round rocks that are slippery and often the cause of a good dunking. I liken wading the Mile to wading the Box Canyon of the Henry's Fork in Idaho.

There is very little bankside structure along the course of this stretch of river, mainly because of the fluctuating water levels. There are some areas where some large rocks are along the bank and provide holding water no matter how low or high the water is, but most of the holding structure is out in the stream itself. In some sections there is plenty of gravel for spawning fish. During the spawning seasons an angler can often spot the redds from the bank. All in all, the Mile has very good water along its entire course; there is very little dead water that does not hold fish at some time.

Accessibility

The Miracle Mile is accessible along its entire length. It is fairly easy to get to from three directions, even though it seems to be out in the middle of nowhere. The drive from the Rawlins area is really interesting because one travels through a moonscape outside Sinclair into a mountainous area with a terrific view of Seminoe Reservoir and the dam. Then there is a descent into a narrow canyon where bighorn sheep are often seen, over a pass with a great view of the plains west of the river, and finally a drop down to the river itself. The road from Sinclair is designated a scenic highway even though the last sections of it are gravel. It is kept open all year and plowed in the winter months. However, if one is going to venture into the canyon in the winter, a four-wheel-drive is necessary because the road can ice up or become snow-packed. The road in the canyon is rather steep in spots, and I have witnessed many ill-equipped vehicles become stuck.

The Mile can also be reached from the north: the access is thirty miles southeast along Highway 220 through the small town of Alcova. The road out of Alcova is the other end of the road out of Sinclair and is about the same distance from the Mile. This road travels through some interesting high plains country. If one travels in the winter a herd of elk that winters in the area may be visible. Again, a four-wheel-drive vehicle is desirable because this road can be drifted over in the winter and mucky in the spring. At times it can be slow going because most of the road is gravel, but it is a fairly good road by Wyoming standards. I keep hearing rumors that the state highway department is eventually going to pave the entire road from Sinclair to Alcova.

The entrance from the east is through the town of Medicine Bow, which lies about twenty miles north of Interstate 80. Take Highway 487 to 77, where there will be a gravel road cutoff to the Mile area. Four-wheel-drives again may be necessary in the winter.

During the summer months, none of these routes should cause any problems other than a possible chip in the windshield because of the gravel. But the winter months are something else and travelers must take precautions. An emergency kit of blankets, water, and food is always a good idea when traveling any road in Wyoming in the winter months. The weather can become dangerous in a very short time.

On the Mile itself, there are accesses along its entire stretch. There is free camping at various sites, with some decent outhouses. However, there is very little firewood, so bring your own if you must. Too many people in the past have hacked away at the standing vegetation—don't add to the problem. Also, the wind here can blow severely. My first experience with spending the night here was in a very small and cheap backpack tent. I woke up in the middle of the night with both sides of my tent slapping me in the face as the wind howled—it made for a very bad night's sleep. Even if it is calm out, stake your tent, lest you find it floating down the river as you are fishing.

Be advised that there are some rattlesnakes in the area that can pose a problem if there are small children in your party. One can see deer, antelope, coyotes, sometimes elk, and even bighorn sheep from the campsites. When the sheep are plentiful it isn't uncommon to see them along the road.

There is a bridge at about the halfway point in the river, over which the road from Sinclair crosses the river on its way to Alcova. The bridge is fairly low to the water, so floating here usually is prevented. A few of my friends use float tubes on the lower end of the Mile when there are sufficient flows. One friend in particular was obsessed with catching a large walleye on a fly, so he would work the lower end from a float tube, walk back upstream, and do it again. There are dirt roads along both sides of the river both upstream and down. This is probably the most accessible seven miles of river in the state.

Management

There appears to be a black hole in knowledge about this stretch of water on the part of the fish and game department. This is not a criticism, because fish and game is in the process of conducting a long-range study so that they may learn more about what actually does happen in this tailwater and the other sections included in the study. The study includes the river from I-80 through Casper and is called the *North Platte River Comprehensive Fisheries Study*.

The study was initiated to evaluate the success of trout-stocking programs. The species and strains of stocked trout that survive best in the wild and that are best suited for each area of water will be identified. This information will allow the department to provide the fisherman with a better fishery.

Trout of various groups will be fitted with different coded-wire tags so that over the next several years they can be recovered by creel census, netting, and electrofishing. Thousands of different groups of fish will be marked. In the next few years, anglers who catch a tagged fish will be able to retrieve the wire tag and from it determine the trout's strain and when and where it was planted.

A tagging crew will tag nearly ten thousand fish a day, about three-quarters of a million trout a year. A full-time biologist has been employed to supervise the study. Plans are to keep the numbers of stocked fish standard for the next three or four years at ten thousand browns, twenty thousand rainbows, and twenty thousand cutthroats. The fish tagged are the five-inch "sub-catchables" or advanced fingerlings.

This study should begin to answer some of the questions that have plagued local clubs for years. According to fish and game, angling pressure has no significant impact on the Mile as a fishery yet. A fish-population estimate is especially difficult on the Mile because of fish migrating back and forth from Pathfinder Reservoir. The various strains of trout that are in the river system all have different spawning times, and getting an accurate count of fish per mile is extremely difficult. So the department has some trouble supporting its claims about angling pressure, at least to the satisfaction of the local clubs that push for special regulations in the form of creel limits or the use only of artificials.

I have noticed a change in the winter fishing over the past few years. I used to catch a good number of smaller fish that were predominantly rainbows, and now my catch is made up mostly of very large brown trout. There has been a creel limit of one brown trout a day for the past few years. That would help explain why there are more fish, but fish and game believes the low water that has caused the length of the Mile to increase has also produced low flows. These low flows mean water that is favorable to brown trout.

All the brown trout in the Mile are wild; they have become self-sustaining, so stocking is no longer necessary. There is a brown trout from Yugoslavia—the Ohrid brown—originally planted in Pathfinder because it had the capability to spawn in a lake, which has become self-sustaining also. In addition to the browns, there are some wild rainbows and four different strains of hatchery fish that are stocked annually. And a small number of cutthroat may be found in the Mile. Walleye have been abundant in the lower reach in the past, especially in the spring when they move into the river to spawn.

The low flows and dewatering of Pathfinder Reservoir have extended the length of the Mile. Because of this, the spawning runs have been short-stopped from their traditional beds. Fish are now spawning in the river much farther downstream. This makes it seem to upstream fishermen that there are less fish in the river during the spawning runs. And the extended Mile has fish more dispersed throughout its nearly doubled distance, again appearing to the upstream fisherman as if there are fewer fish in the river.

The low flows have produced some negative effects on the fishery. They inhibit natural reproduction, possibly because of the reduction in oxygen saturation levels. The low flows have also left some of the food-producing riffles high and dry, killing the insects that would normally abound there and resulting in a loss of habitat. On the other hand, insect life is starting to take hold in the downstream sections.

Seasonal Changes in Fishing

Tailwater fisheries are unique in the sense that very few major changes take place in them over the course of a year. There is no runoff period to contend with in the spring and no frozen water to wait out. The changes that do occur are a little more subtle. The temperatures in a tailwater do not have the wide swings that are normally found in other parts of the river system—the sections that freeze over in the winter and rise into the seventy-degree range in the heat of the summer. Tailwaters have a narrower band of change that makes them fishable when other sections are either too hot or too cold. This uniform range of temperatures helps support an insect population throughout the year and turns the water into a bug factory, much to the benefit of the trout.

Although different food sources become available at different times of the year, there is a constant abundance of food in a tailwater. Probably the most notable and abundant source is the scud, a freshwater crustacean that is often misnamed freshwater shrimp (see illustration on page 152). Scuds are the single most important food source year-round in the Mile. They are grayish golden olive in color and vary in size from very tiny to about an inch long. Throughout the year the majority seem to be a specific size because they seem to develop at the same rate. In some months the majority of scuds will be about #16 and in other months a #10 or #12. A quick kick-screening will aid the angler in determining what size to imitate.

Over my years of fishing on the Mile it became evident that one of the hottest patterns is a rusty-orange-colored scud. I'm really not sure

how this evolved: more than
likely it came about when
someone gave one a try because it had worked on a different river. In all my years of
kick-screening on the Mile, I
have never seen an orange
scud. Then a fishing buddy

stopped by my house and excitedly whipped out a collection vial to
show me. It contained a natural orange scud he screened on the Mile.
At last, verification that they do exist. Patterns tied to imitate this oddity
are deadly throughout most of the year.

Fish can be caught at any time of the year using a scud imitation,
even if there is an abundance of other insects, as in a major hatch period.
The trout may become selective to some other insect for a brief time,
but not all the trout in a given spot are ultraselective. I have caught trout
on scud imitations whose stomach samples held nothing but midge pupa.
Apparently eating scuds is such a habit that passing up the easy scud
just doesn't occur very often.

This is not to say that a scud will take fish every day in every spot;
unfortunately, it's not that easy. If fish are rising to a hatching dun on
the surface, then a scud imitation might not take fish, especially if it
is fished on the bottom. The spawning fish that are sitting on redds worry-
ing away intruders and any other perceived threats will probably not
take a scud imitation. But generally, a selection of scud imitations in
various sizes and shades is necessary for success on the Mile.

Spring (March, April, and May)

Spring has always seemed to me to be a transitional period on the
Mile. There seems to be a slowdown in the fishing, and although I have
had some great days fishing in the early spring, March and early April
are traditionally slow for me. I think that there is a prespawn period
in the spring when fish are not feeding heavily or are not holding in
the usual places. In looking back over my years of notes, the days when
I caught significant numbers of fish usually included a major hatch of
midges or *Baetis*, and then most of the fish have been on the smallish
side. The large fish I have caught over the years have been few, and

some of them I can attribute to a defensive reaction to a streamer during the spawn. Some were large browns taken on egg patterns. A friend of mine caught a seven-pound rainbow in a shallow riffle on a black Woolly Bugger in March one year that was probably defending its territory during the spawn. On the other hand, I can remember a six-pound rainbow I caught experimenting with a tiny midge larva pattern. There are still large fish to be caught in the spring, but my experience tells me they are not as common as they are in other seasons.

In March the weather brings some of those super-nice days that tease one out to play. Many people, especially those who choose not to fish in the winter months, have that itch to get out and fish, so the crowds begin to appear on the Mile. If the flows are low, the first few people in a given spot have the best opportunity to catch fish. The more a spot gets hammered, the less likely a person is to have success.

The warmer days of the spring begin to warm the water temperatures over the course of the day and seem to trigger the premier hatch of the early spring—the midge. Although there is a significant hatch in the late winter months, early spring brings the best hatches. Often there are so many midges on the water that trout will rise to clusters of these tiny insects rather than to individuals. This midge hatch has always been a tough nut to crack because fish seemed to rise randomly and not in a rhythmically patterned manner. A few techniques and patterns have solved this problem and can turn the usual frustrating day into a successful day. These midges are tiny—often as small as #26—and most of the fish seem to key on the pupa most of the time. The pupae suspend themselves in the surface film prior to emerging and become relatively vulnerable to the fish. Trout will feed on the pupa as it rises from the bottom, during the ascent, and in the surface film, so there are more opportunities for a fish to feed. The larva are tiny and can be found along the bottom in the drift, and although I have caught fish using a larva imitation, my success with it has been marginal at best. The adult can only be found on the surface for limited periods of time (until it flies off), and if the wind is blowing hard, as it often does, the fish usually do not key on them.

Many times a fisherman will see fish apparently rising to adults when they are actually taking pupae. In the past, fish would randomly rise from the middle sections of the stream in slow, deep glides to occasionally

A seven-pound spring rainbow. (Photo courtesy Steve Hays)

take a midge from the surface film or the surface. These fish were very difficult to catch because one could not time a cast to the rise, and the fish would never seem to rise in the same place twice. Drifting a dry fly or even a pupa over the area was generally unproductive. After reading Sylvester Nemes's book, *The Soft-Hackled Fly Addict,* I designed a small soft-hackle I thought would resemble a midge pupa. The result could not have been better. The black soft-hackle has become my number-one fly when I midge the Mile. The beauty of it is that a total idiot could fish it and still be successful (that's my kind of fly). I get great pleasure demonstrating its effectiveness to unbelievers.

The technique is so simple that novices have no difficulty using it. A cast, which does not have to be perfect or particularly accurate, is made in the general area of rising fish, and the fly is not manipulated at all. Just let it swing in the current in the old wet-fly swing. The technique is more effective if the fly can swing from an area of current to the slower, still areas along the banks. For the more sophisticated fisherman, individually rising fish can be worked by casting far enough upstream so that the fly will swing right in front of the fish.

Solid hookups are difficult because of the angle of the strike. The angler is upstream of the fish, and if too violent a strike is made, the hook is pulled up and away from the fish. More solid hookups can be had by slowly lifting the rod and tightening the line. Any quick movement of the rod will result in a missed fish. Most strikes are felt, but there are many that go undetected because the fish generally strike in an upstream direction, causing no tension in the line unless they solidly hook themselves. By holding the rod with the tip elevated, one can watch the line from where it hangs from the tip to where it meets the water's surface. When a fish takes the soft-hackle, a noticeable hesitation or flip in the line can be perceived. At that time, slowly lift the rod and tighten the line. This technique does work (see illustration on page 156).

When fish are rising in a patterned manner, then other, more traditional, techniques can be used successfully. Any traditional small adult midge pattern can be floated over rising fish, or a greased leader and pupa can be used with good results. One of the better patterns to use in these circumstances is the Palomino Midge in either the adult or pupa configuration. On those days when the wind is not blowing very hard, midge fish can be awesome.

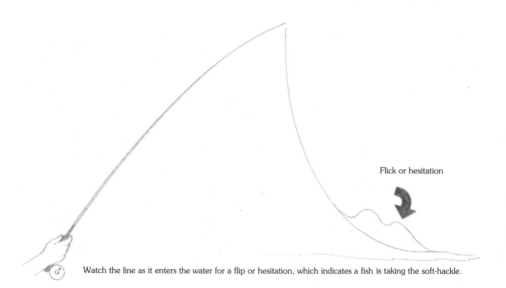

Watch the line as it enters the water for a flip or hesitation, which indicates a fish is taking the soft-hackle.

Flick or hesitation

The Mile is one of the few places where I have noticed fish feeding on spent midges in the drift. The more common occurrence is for fish to take spent midges as they pack together in back eddies or scum lines. This happens on the Mile also. In the late afternoon one can see thick scum lines of midges along the shore in the slower stretches. Often, large fish can be spotted cruising these scum lines, sipping clumps of midge bodies inches from the bank. These fish are extremely wary and very difficult to take. In order to have any chance at them, the angler needs to position himself out in the stream, or if that isn't possible, far enough downstream so as not to spook the fish. A bankside approach or upstream approach will terrify the fish. A cast should be made to the stream side of the scum line and fish, and it should be a delicate one (see illustration on page 157). This is technical fishing in the extreme.

The fish that take spent midges in the drift are somewhat easier to catch and, to me, something of an oddity. I have witnessed fish on spring creeks taking spent midges in the middle of the afternoon, but I haven't seen this in too many other places. The fish on the Mile do seem to key on this stage of the midge in the late afternoon on windless days. Usually they hold in the tailouts of pools and sip these dead bugs off the

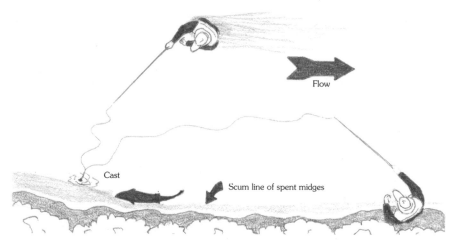

Cast to the stream side of a fish that is feeding on spent midges along a bank.

surface, much like fish taking Trico spinners. They are fished in the same manner as one would fish any spinner fall: using dead-drifted patterns with absolutely no drag. Usually by the time this occurs I am shivering as the sun gets low on the horizon and somewhat sloppy in my casting, so I end up spooking more fish than I hook, but it can be a pleasant way of ending a day of fishing nevertheless.

As the year moves into April, the midge fishing is still strong and the spawning run of rainbows begins, followed by a spawning run of cutthroats. At this time a hodgepodge of fishing takes place. Fish that are in the spawning mode are usually not interested in eating but can be coerced into striking something that simply ticks them off. Streamers fit the bill nicely for this type of fishing. Once fish that appear to be spawning are located, a well-placed streamer can result in some startlingly savage strikes. Fishing over spawning fish is a dilemma that every individual fisherman has to deal with. Is it ethical (or is that politically correct?) for an angler to take advantage of these fish and possibly overstress them, or is the temptation to take some large fish just too great? I leave the resolution up to you.

During the spawn, something more important to the angler occurs: nonspawning fish will often hold below the redds and suck in the eggs that drift by. The old glow bug or egg pattern dead-drifted works well for these fish. A pattern I have had success with is a downsized version of the Nuclear Egg pattern, in about #14—after all, these fish are not salmon or steelhead. Even if redds are not identified, the pattern seems to take fish in most sections of the river. Fish seem to look for drifting eggs.

At one point, April 12 marked the prime time for the walleye fishermen. Since the recent years of low water, this date is not so important for walleye because snagging has been eliminated and the traditional water does not hold as many fish as before. A friend of mine, who was obsessed with catching a large walleye on a fly, would fish grotesquely garish patterns that resembled stuff one would take to Alaska. He used a fast-sinking line and would work these gaudy patterns along the bottom of the slower pools in the lower reaches of the Mile. He did catch a few walleye, but the surprise was the number of large cutthroats he caught in the process.

As we move into May, the midge fishing begins to wane but the overall quality of fishing in general begins to pick up. *Baetis* species have taken hold as the prime surface action at this time. These tiny mayflies provide for some good dry-fly fishing because fish are keyed to the surface. Let me clarify this. In years where the flows in the Mile are fairly constant for extended periods, the fish have the chance to key to the surface. If there are wide water-level fluctuations on a daily basis, the fish never do key to the surface because they are always on the move and cannot establish a feeding lane.

A #18 Blue Dun or Blue-Winged Olive works well for the BWO (*Baetis*) adult and a #18 Pheasant Tail for the nymph. Fish will often become selective to the emerger during this hatch, so a floating nymph or emerging nymph pattern should be used. One technique that can cover both bases is to fish an adult pattern with an emerger (see illustration on page 159). The dun will act as a strike indicator for the emerger, which floats in the surface film.

One year when the flows were very constant, the *Baetis* hatch was so plentiful and regular that gulls actually sat on the water where trout would normally hold and picked these insects off the surface. Of course, no trout in its right mind would hold near the surface next to a large bird, so the gulls took the prime water away from the trout.

I have been discussing surface action, but nymph fishing is far and above the most consistent technique for taking fish at all times of the year

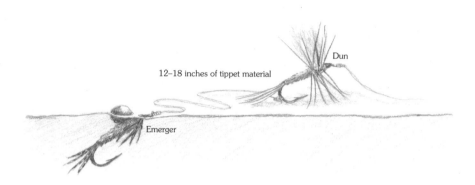

12–18 inches of tippet material

Dun

Emerger

Dun-to-Emerger Setup

on the Mile. It is not the most glamorous way to fish, and it doesn't have that artistic look to it. But the majority, by far, of the fish taken on the Mile have been caught on a nymph. This is the time of year when the mayfly nymphs and caddis larvae have grown large enough that the fish make more use of them as a food source.

The bottom of the river is literally alive with insects. The scuds are ever present and the caddis and mayflies present a buffet table for the trout. Fishing small nymph patterns in #14 and #16 is very often deadly. I can recall numerous fifty-fish days in May when I was using small nymphs. I use my own PMD pattern, but a Hare's Ear-type fly is just as effective.

Early Summer (End of May to Beginning of July) and Midsummer (July and August)

I am lumping all these summer months together because what happens in the beginning of the summer continues through to the end. This is the time of plenty, because most of the mayflies and caddisflies mature and hatch now. There is a very wide assortment of bugs and I will discuss only those significant to the angler.

Nymphing the Mile.

There are a few food items that should be discussed because they are of some importance to the nymph fisherman. Besides the scuds, which are still very abundant, the mayfly nymphs, and the caddis larvae, there is an aquatic worm that is somewhat abundant in the bottom drift, especially when the flows are high. These worms are a few inches long and are reddish or brown; they can be imitated with a San Juan Worm. They are not as plentiful as are those found on the Big Horn River in Montana, but fish here do feed on them.

Another insect the high flows stir up is the cranefly larva. It is not found in great numbers, but stomach samples indicate that fish do feed on it, and a friend of mine regularly fishes an imitation with success. A rather unusual insect, a *Parargyractis* species larva, is also very abundant in some stretches of the Mile. This is a moth larva that is best imitated with a #8 or #10 thin-bodied olive Woolly Worm. (Finally, something a Woolly Worm imitates.) The Woolly Worm is one of the first flies a beginning fly tier tries, and I'll bet most of you still have more than you'll ever use.

The summer months bring all the traditional bugs with the attendant traditional fishing techniques. Caddisflies make their appearance in the early summer and continue into the fall. As the fish key on the caddis, one can often observe the slashing, showy riseforms typical of a caddis hatch. Over the course of the summer there are two periods of the day when caddis are important to the fisherman: late morning and evening. The late-morning hatch may bring periods of frenzied feeding by the fish, but this is not usually the case. I think the wind may play a major role in this or, because caddis normally emerge in the riffles, spotting the riseforms may be difficult and they may go undetected. A splashy rise in a calmer section of stream is very noticeable, but one in a riffled area is tough to see unless the fish comes out of the water.

The late-morning hatch isn't the kind where whole sections of the river are alive with feeding fish. If an angler will work the riffled area with a caddis dry or emerger, success can be had; better still, work the riffle with an adult pattern and an emerger pattern, allowing the dry to float drag-free, then letting it swing in the current with the wet-fly swing. Many fishermen overlook this fishing because they do not recognize that the hatch is taking place. The interesting thing is that during the summer months fish can be caught using many different techniques, so it is easy to miss some of the hatches or emergences as they occur. So many insects become available to fish that unless the fish become ultraselective to a particular one they can be caught on a wide variety of offerings.

Evening caddis fishing can be excellent, especially if the wind is not too strong. Many caddis will return to the river to lay eggs by diving into the water, swimming to the bottom, then returning to the surface, or simply by dipping into the surface film. This is the prime time for a swimming caddis pattern swung in the current.

An interesting technique a buddy of mine uses almost exclusively in the summer months is a double fly setup. He uses a long rod, floating line, and two flies about eighteen inches apart. He will cast quartering downstream and let the flies swing in the wet-fly-swing style. The difference in his technique is that he will hold the rod high in the air so that the top fly daps occasionally onto the surface as both flies swing in the current, with the bottom fly swimming across the current. This way he covers both the swimming caddis and the dipping caddis. It is a deadly technique and he does take some amazing fish using it.

The little yellow stonefly or yellow sally is, in the opinion of some longtime fishermen on the Mile, the predominant summer hatch. It is often mistaken for a caddis hatch by many people because these flies are about the same size as most caddis and about the same shape. They have some of the same habits as well, particularly when they swarm over the water's surface and dip into the water to lay eggs. Of course, they are not caddis and can be identified by their wings, which lie flat over their bodies rather than in the caddis tentlike shape. The bodies are yellow, very often with an orange butt section caused by egg masses. They return to the stream to deposit their eggs in the late afternoon and evening, much the same as the caddis do. Even though they are confused with caddis, a specific pattern imitating them isn't neces-sary—any of the lighter caddis patterns will do the job.

However, the nymph of the little yellow stonefly is a very different creature than a caddis larva and pupa. Whereas a caddis larva will pupate and rise to the surface to emerge into an adult, usually in riffled water, the yellow sally nymph will drift from the riffles into calm shallow water, where it will swim to shore, or anything that protrudes from the surface of the water, crawl up, and hatch out into an adult. This usually takes place in the midafternoon.

The good news is that it's relatively easy to fish this action. As a matter of fact, many novice fly fishers catch fish using a technique that imitates this action without even knowing it. Usually, a beginning nymph fisherman will have trouble controlling his line when dead-drifting a nymph along the bottom. He will spend more time fishing the lower end of the drift, where there is usually considerable drag on the fly that causes it to swim across the current instead of drifting with it. The swim-ming nymph usually ends up downstream from the angler in a relatively calm area of water, where the angler will either let it hang for a while or begin stripping it back. Any nymphing veteran would already have recast for the next drift. This semisloppy way of nymphing almost exactly imitates the actions of the little yellow stonefly nymph as it drifts down the stream and swims to the bank in the slower water.

There are many other stoneflies present in the Mile, including the large *Pteronarcys* species and the golden stone, but not in sufficient num-bers to get excited about. A few may be seen fluttering about, and an occasional fish will take one, but they are few and far between. I bring them to your attention because many people have taken fish using stonefly nymph patterns or a Halfback.

Mayflies are abundant in the summer months, and the pale morning dun is the most abundant. When the flows are constant, this hatch can provide excellent fishing; when the flows are very high or fluctuating, however, not much happens. One summer when the water was slightly out of its banks, a major PMD hatch came off in huge amounts. There were so many adults on the water that there wasn't a six-inch-square of surface that didn't have a PMD on it. I got excited and prepared for one of those killer days, but I never did see a fish rise, and believe me, I looked real hard.

In the late-morning hours the PMD nymphs begin to ascend to the surface to hatch. Prior to this some extremely good nymph fishing can be had with a PMD imitation or a small, #16, mayfly nymph pattern like the Gold-Ribbed Hare's Ear. The pattern I use almost exclusively also served double duty as a pretty good imitation of the ever-so-present scud, at least in size and color. In looking back over my records, I see the overwhelming majority of fish I have caught on the Mile over the course of the year have been taken on a #14 PMD nymph. It happens to be a pattern I have a lot of confidence in, so I fish it most often, which probably accounts for the numbers of fish I have caught.

The evening will bring a PMD spinner fall that probably gets overlooked because of the yellow sallies and caddis action. A Rusty Spinner in #14 will take fish that are looking to the surface for spentwings in the calmer waters.

There are many other mayflies that hatch out over the summer months, but none hatch in numbers great enough to get too excited about. The fish certainly don't. The good news is that anglers working different mayfly imitations have a good chance of picking up fish.

Toward the middle of August the water begins to turn very murky, and there is a fair amount of junk in the drift. The first time I witnessed this was when I moved West. In the early part of the summer I had fantastic fishing, then had to go away for a few months. All I could think of was returning and fishing the Mile, but when I did return the water was up and discolored and stayed that way into October. This is a common occurrence caused by one of two things, according to the locals. It is either Seminoe Reservoir turning over, or the result of the upstream runoff finally working its way through the reservoir. Or it could be something else entirely. The result is the same: very poor fishing. I know people still fish in these conditions and catch fish, but I usually head for different waters.

Summer is the time of year when most people are out on the stream, so the crowds are something that needs to be tolerated. Those who have expectations of relatively secluded fishing on the Mile in the summer might end up very angry. The guy who tailors his expectations to meet the conditions usually is the guy who enjoys himself. Type A personalities might find the Mile a little tough to deal with in the summer, especially on weekends.

Fall (September, October, and November)

Early September still finds the Mile with murky waters as the turnover or runoff continues. Fish can still be had and are taken by a fair amount of people using bright nymphs and streamers.

In some years the water begins to clear toward the end of September and in others not until the middle of October. When the water begins to clear, the fishing obviously begins to pick up. The clearing water finds the *Baetis* species have established themselves as the premier mayflies and any overcast day will bring a major hatch. The weather can begin to be on the nasty side—it can and usually does snow sometime in September. There are still caddis hatches to fish and the nymph fishing is still strong.

October begins the prime time on the Mile, even though it might still be murky. It is a prespawn period for the brown trout, who seem to put on the feedbag in preparation for the winter months. The rainbows also exhibit feeding binges (much like me when I'm watching a football game). Fishing with scud imitations is very good, as is using other nymph patterns. Streamer fishing picks up, and this is a time to use all the Platte River Specials one has. Many spin fishermen can be observed fishing a Special above a flexible weight and seem to have good success. Working some of the faster water with a sinking-tip line and streamer is an effective way to fly fish at this time of year.

Browns seem to prefer the more oxygenated water of the riffles and faster runs. It must have something to do with the spawning urge, because when the rainbows are spawning the same thing appears to happen. Some truly large fish are caught at this time. I watched an angler hook a large brown in relatively shallow fast water; the size of the fish, force of the water, and relative unskilled handling brought him quite a way downstream during the fight before he was able to land it. It turned out to be a brown measuring over thirty inches and probably weighing in the teens.

The crowds thin out somewhat because of the bad weather that can hit and because many of the locals are out hunting. Usually only the hardcores are on the stream, and the fishing is usually intense. This is not to say that there aren't crowds—too many people know about the quality of fishing here for an angler to have the place to himself. But if one can get on the Mile when the weather is not optimum, some fabulous fishing without too much competition can be experienced.

Most of the browns are finished spawning or will be finished spawning in November and begin then to take nourishment. There may be some leftover *Baetis* action, but most of the fishing will be nymph-fishing with scuds the primary food source. By this time, most of the other fishermen have taken off and the Mile is relatively crowd-free. Usually weekdays are good times to fish.

Winter (December, January, and February)

This is cold-weather fishing in the extreme! Technology has brought about a development in fabrics and clothing that can efficiently keep a body warm without bulk. (The person who developed neoprene waders ought to have a shrine built in his honor so winter fishermen can pay their respects.) The days of wearing regular waders over layers and layers of binding clothing only to end up freezing anyway are pretty much over. But it can still be on the chilly side here if one isn't prepared. I find that long johns under a fleece sweatsuit and a good Gore-Tex windbreaker and neoprene waders keep me comfortable. A hat to keep the head warm, wading shoes that aren't tight (loose-fitting shoes are very important in keeping feet comfortable), and a pair of gloves— either wool or neoprene—are also necessary for winter fishing. The gloves do not have to keep your hands dry, but they do need to retain body heat—there is nothing worse than trying to fish with cold hands. A complete change of warm clothes should always accompany you on a winter fishing trip to the Mile.

Cold-weather fishing does strange things to one's body. Hands do not want to do what the brain tells them to; tying a knot or unraveling a tangle takes much more time with stiff fingers. The best way to untangle a line in the cold is to approach it slowly and systematically, then begin cursing, clip it off, go back to the vehicle, and tie on a new leader in the warmth and comfort of the truck fortified with a cup of hot coffee. When wading, the feet get somewhat stiff and seem to have a mind of their own. I have taken many a nosedive because my feet decided they didn't want to do the same thing I did, like step over a rock. I suppose there were many times in the winter when my friends and I were borderline hypothermic without realizing it. Steve, my longtime friend and fishing partner, has quit fishing in the winter because of the cold. He used to come with me in the winter and bring a book to read because he spent so much time in the truck warming up he figured he should have something to do. One trip found him in my truck so much with the heater running that I had serious doubts about having enough gas to make it back to town.

Icing of the guides is a serious problem in the winter, and I wish I knew how to prevent it. I've tried everything I've ever read about preventing it and found nothing that works.

I've been carrying on about the rigors of winter fishing, and you are probably wondering why I bother. Big fish, that's why. In the last few years, on nearly every winter trip I have made, someone in my party at least hooked a fish over five pounds. There have been many winter days on the Mile when *every* fish hooked was in that class.

Winter fishing is almost entirely nymph fishing, and the scud is the primary imitation. Over the course of the winter the size of the scuds increases to almost an inch.

The large fish seem to hold in slightly slower water that is well oxygenated from a riffle or fast water above. They also seem to hold in pods. If a pod of large fish can be located, an excellent day is in store.

There is a fair amount of midge fishing in the month of December, at least until a very cold snap occurs. After the cold snap the midges seem to wait until the days begin to warm up a little before they hatch in any numbers.

Toward the end of December and into the first part of January, a spawning run of a late-spawning rainbow species begins. We found this by accident one year when a smart friend noticed that many of the fish we caught had eggs or milt spilling out of them. This spawning run takes place around the Christmas holidays.

If the weather holds in January (by this I mean if there hasn't yet been a week of below-zero temperatures), the fishing continues to be excellent. If a very cold snap occurs, then it takes a while for the quality of fishing to pick up again. In those years that have waves of very cold weather, the fishing will remain on the slow side throughout the month until the weather begins to let up. Nymphing with scuds is still the ticket in January after the spawn, and if the weather isn't too bad, midges will still provide top-water action. A couple of years ago my very first fish of the year, taken on January 1, was a rainbow that went slightly over five pounds.

February, according to the department of fish and game, is the prime month for catching a very large fish. The weather begins to moderate somewhat as the days begin to lengthen—it can be downright pleasant in February. Nymph-fishing with scuds is still the ticket for successful fishing, and the warmer temperatures start the real good midge fishing. In the years with a good supply of smaller fish, many can be taken on midges, so much so that one year I brought my 4-weight specifically for them. The water was low and I figured that I could have some fun playing the little fish (ten to fourteen inches). I was using a black soft-hackle and caught a few when I saw a decent fish rise out in the current. I cast to it, and it immediately took the fly. After a rather protracted battle a seven-pound brown lay gasping at my feet.

I find that as we progress to the end of February the fishing begins to slow down, especially for the larger fish. On some days, if it wasn't for the little fish caught midging, things would be dismal.

It should be noted that during the winter months the wind blows at an average speed of thirty miles an hour. Wind does some interesting things to fly lines and leaders, especially those weighted leaders used for nymphing. I swear I could not tie some of the knots in my leader the wind does if I tried.

Tackle requirements on the Mile depend on many factors: water flow, time of year, technique used. I think that if an angler had one nine-foot 6-weight rod set up, any winter fishing situation could be handled. A consideration is that some of the water in the Mile is quite strong and some of the fish are quite large—an outfit that can handle that combination should be considered. One tackle requirement I find crucial is a reel with a very good drag system. I learned how to rely on a properly set drag when I used to fish for saltwater species, so I trust good reels with good drags more so than many fly fishers. I lose very few fish because of poor drag.

Locally Effective Patterns

Rusty Orange Scud

Hook: 10-16
Thread: Orange
Tails: Orange Krystal Flash
Ribbing: Copper wire
Shellback: Strip of pearlescent
            Flashabou sheet
Body: Rusty orange dubbing
Legs: Picked-out dubbing

Olive Scud

Hook: 10-16
Thread: Olive
Tail: Olive mallard-flank-feather
            fibers
Ribbing: Monofilament
Shellback: Strip of pearlescent Flasha-
            bou sheet
Body: Golden olive dubbing
Legs: Picked-out dubbing

Black Soft-Hackle

Hook: 14-18
Thread: Black
Ribbing: Silver wire
Abdomen: Black thread
Thorax: Peacock herl
Hackle: Grouse soft hackle

Little Yellow Stonefly Nymph

Hook: 12-14
Thread: Olive
Tail: Boar's hair or paint-brush bristles
Abdomen: Barred mallard flank wrapped around hook shank
Thorax: Hare's ear dubbing
Wingcase: Barred mallard flank pulled over thorax
Antennae: Same as tail

Yellow Sally

Hook: 12-16
Thread: Yellow
Tip: Red-orange poly dubbing
Body: Yellow poly dubbing
Wing: Tan elk hair tied flat over body
Hackle: Ginger, trimmed top and bottom
Head: Yellow thread

Nuclear Egg

Hook: 14
Thread: Fluorescent orange
Body: Fluorescent orange yarn
           or dubbing
Wing: White Antron yarn tied so
           it sheaths body

Palomino Midge Pupa

Hook: 16-22
Thread: Black
Thorax: Black or dark gray
            Ultra-Chenille
Adbomen: Black dubbing or peacock
            herl
Wingcase: White Z-lon pulled
            forward
Antennae: White Z-lon

Palomino Midge Adult

Hook: 16-22
Thread: Black
Thorax: Black or dark gray Ultra-
            Chenille
Abdomen: Black dubbing or peacock
Hackle: Grizzly or black

Other Effective Patterns

Midge larva
Griffith's Gnat
Spent midge
Brassie
Caddis larva
Caddis emergent pupa
Diving caddis
Elk Hair Caddis
Bucktail caddis
Prince Nymph
Red Fox Squirrel Nymph
Rusty Spinner
Pale Morning Dun thorax
PMD

Gold-Ribbed Hare's Ear
Blue Dun
Blue-Winged Olive
Baetis emerger
Adams
Flashback Nymph
Halfback
Olive Woolly Worm
Cranefly larva
San Juan Worm
Glo-Bug
Platte River Specials
Flash-A-Bugger
Clouser's Deep Minnow

9

Gray Reef to Casper

The Gray Reef area is a tailwater fishery and remains fishable through the year. This stretch of river actually has several tailwater areas that occur in the upper reaches of the section as the river flows into the town of Casper. The river in the Miracle Mile section dumps into Pathfinder Reservoir, where it flows into Alcova Reservoir by way of Fremont Canyon. A good deal of water flows through a tunnel that feeds a power plant on the way to Alcova.

The Fremont Canyon area could become a tailwater fishery if a few problems were overcome. The Wyoming Department of Fish and Game, the Bureau of Reclamation, and local fishing clubs are all striving to work out the difficulties in order to establish and maintain a 300 cfs flow, which would enable a Blue Ribbon fishery to be established. The unique element here is that the Bureau of Reclamation is working with other agencies and clubs to establish this fishery, which is a major change in philosophy for it. The near future may see another small tailwater established here with management practices that actually benefit the angler.

The river enters Alcova Reservoir, where it backs up into a still-water fishery. It exits Alcova to become a very short tailwater before entering Gray Reef, which is an afterbay or small regulatory dam. This section of river experiences some major fluctuations from almost no water to heavy flows on its mile or so journey. Fish and game uses this section to dump its excess brood culls of Eagle Lake rainbows, usually in January. Obviously, this provides some decent fishing for some rather large trout. Beside the brood culls, there are some huge fish in this section that probably grew up in the Gray Reef Reservoir, at least before the water level dropped. The summer has some great hatches, and many of the locals have learned where and when to fish here. When the water is wildly fluctuating the fishing is poor.

This chapter will discuss the section of river from the outflow of Gray Reef Reservoir to the town of Casper. On this forty-five-mile trek the river makes a gradual change from tailwater to free flows, from trophy water to an average fishery, and from Blue Ribbon trout water to one where other species have been planted.

Topography

This section of river flows through ranchland that has been carved out of sagebrush. The terrain is somewhat flat, with mountains to the south. As the river nears the town of Casper it flows through a narrows section that is flanked by foothill-like rises called Bessemer and Coal mountains.

Beginning at the small town of Alcova, the river flows to Casper. Alcova is a community comprised mainly of summer homes, cabins, and trailers. There is a small grocery store–gas station and a bar that serves a decent hamburger. The city of Casper is Wyoming's largest and has all the amenities a big city can offer. Museums, shopping, restaurants, and plenty of motels are at the disposal of visiting anglers.

Water Characteristics

The forty-five or so miles of this stretch can be divided into two different sections: the upper stretch, which is a tailwater, and the lower section, which is not. There is a transitional section that is somewhat affected by the upstream tailwater, but only a little. This section may be much slower to freeze in the winter than the downstream sections are, but it *will* eventually freeze. The upstream stretches of the tailwater remain open all year. The lower reaches are subject to runoff in the spring, when many of its tributaries dump snowmelt into the river. As the river flows downstream, the good trout habitat progressively declines and the classification changes from Class I, or Blue Ribbon, to Class II, or Red Ribbon, water. The break in the classification is at Bessemer Bend, roughly thirty miles from Gray Reef. The eastern edge of Casper marks the beginning of Class III water.

The first few miles of river in the Gray Reef section have, to my way of thinking, the most interesting water. I like the ratio of riffles to pools—it appears to be greater here than anywhere else on this stretch. There is more character to the water, with a variety of water speeds and currents to fish. As one progresses downstream the riffles become farther and farther apart, eventually turning into an almost straight shot with very little character: the streambed practically levels out as it approaches Casper.

There are some channeled areas, but these are few and far between. Where they do occur they provide for good current edges, different water speeds, small riffles, and deeper pockets as the water braids around the islands and comes back together. The river does meander quite a bit, forming good inside bends for the nymph fisherman. There are grassy banks where fish will hold and feed when there are insects on the surface. Bottom structure ranges from a small rubble in some of the riffles to a silty muck in the slow glides. Pea gravel is available to the spawning fish but mostly occurs in the upper reaches.

This area of river has experienced a good deal of spawning and food-producing-habitat degradation in the past five or so years because of near-drought weather conditions. The lower flows of the dry years has caused siltation to become a major problem, especially in areas of the river downstream from any tributary. The occasional violent thunderstorms wash sediment into the river that will silt in food-producing riffles and cover eggs, killing both insects and eggs. The low flows do not have sufficient force to cleanse these silted areas. The University of Wyoming is conducting a study to determine how much water flow is needed to flush the river of sediment and preserve the habitat. Bates Creek is one of the worst tributaries for muddying the water, and as the river flows closer to Casper, more and more tributaries dump more and more silt into the water.

The river has some very good habitat as it winds through the city of Casper. Fish and game tells me there are more trout per mile in town than in the fabled Snake River. Supposedly there are eight thousand pounds of trout per mile in Casper.

Because this entire stretch is affected by the dams, the flows fluctuate over the course of a season. Generally, flows in a summer with normal water volumes near the 3,000 cfs mark and slow down in the fall

The river downstream of the dam.

and winter months to around 1,500 cfs. Both numbers vary a bit with water calls and weather conditions but, unlike the Miracle Mile, flows here do not rise and fall too drastically on a day-to-day basis. Water levels are fairly consistent in the winter and summer because Gray Reef Dam regulates the water released from Alcova Reservoir. The flows usually increase for the summer irrigators around the fifteenth of April and shut down around the fifteenth of October. These dates are only generalities—they do change from year to year.

Accessibility

Public access and recreational sites along this portion of river comprise more than two hundred acres of riverfront, making it one of the more accessible for the wading or bank fisherman. The floating fisherman will find the intervals of accessibility convenient for getting out of the boat to fish, lunch, or rest. Public areas are fairly well marked with blue signs, and private sections are marked with red signs. Camping is permitted at the BLM and county-administered access areas. There are tent and trailer sites at the Gray Reef access area.

At the outflow of Gray Reef Dam, one can launch a boat from a concrete ramp, erect a tent, or set up a trailer in the first of the major public landing and parking areas. Many anglers walk this stretch because during low flows one can wade across the river to fish the opposite bank. A short distance downstream is another public access, called Pete's Draw, with no facilities other than a spot on the road for fishermen to stop and fish. It's close enough to the dam that anglers there don't have to go very far to fish. The next access downriver is a BLM site called Ledge Creek, which has very limited vehicle access but is a good area for floating anglers to get out of their boats.

The next major launch site is the Lusby public fishing area, which is off a dirt road about nine miles downstream. There is no concrete ramp. This is probably the most popular take-out because of the distance from Gray Reef. Bank and wade fishermen will find plenty of water to fish in this section.

Downstream from Lusby is the Bolten Creek access, which is a BLM site that can be reached by a dirt road just east of Government Bridge. Government Bridge itself is the third major launch site and access area. It lies just off Highway 220 at the bridge and can accommodate a float fisherman with its dirt ramp.

Immediately west of the bridge is a road that leads to the Clarkson Hill access, another BLM site, and the beginning of almost four miles of river accessibility—it joins up with the next access on the south side of the river. This access is called By the Way, and there is a road from Highway 220 to its parking area. Farther downstream is another access site with very limited vehicle accessibility—Gray Cliff. Most of this access is on the north bank of the river. These limited access areas lead to the Sechrist public fishing area, which includes about half a mile of streambank on both sides of the river, a road to the south bank, a parking area, double outhouses, and a concrete boat ramp. Private property is clearly marked with signs.

A little farther downstream is a pedestrian access, the Schmitt easement at the mouth of Cottonwood Creek on the south side of the river. Adjacent to this property downstream is the Bessemer Mountain site, which has no vehicle access but which can be reached by the walking fisherman from the Schmitt easement. The Bessemer site is on the north side of the river.

The next major launch area is a key access point for float fishermen: Bessemer Bend Historic Site. Located at the Bessemer Bend Bridge, it can be reached by Highway 220. There is a parking area, but improvements are scheduled for the access road and launch area. A couple miles downstream is another BLM site on the north side of the river. It is a large square tract, but only a corner of it adjoins the river.

As one enters the city of Casper, there is a major public area at the junction of Mills Spur Road and Highway 220. This area has a launch facility and is a good take-out area for float fishermen. Farther on in town is a site at Patterson Park with limited facilities. Throughout town there are other areas where a wading fisherman can wet a line.

Obviously, accessibility is not too much of a problem on this stretch of river. In areas that are not open to the public, ranchers may grant permission to an angler who takes the time to stop by and ask politely. It should be remembered that the landowner does own the bottom of the river, so a floating angler needs to have permission to get out of the boat on private land.

There are two fly shops in Casper, and shuttle service may be arranged through at least one of them. Fly shops are somewhat of a rarity in Wyoming, especially in comparison to other states, so these are definite assets.

Management Practices

Wyoming Fish and Game stocks this section of river on an annual basis. They release 100,000 Eagle Lake rainbows, 100,000 Kamloops rainbows, and 20,000 stream-strain rainbows every year, and 50,000 Snake River cutthroats every other year. These fish are scattered from Gray Reef to the city of Casper. Besides these stocked fish there is a healthy population of wild rainbows and brown trout. In this tailwater environment some fish grow to trophy proportions. In addition to the wild and stocked fish, Casper's local fly-fishing club, The Wyoming Flycasters, in conjunction with fish and game and the Bureau of Reclamation, have installed a Vibert trout-egg-hatching box at the Gray Reef Dam. They loaded 40,000 cutthroat eggs and have had a forty percent hatch.

Because of the tailwater, the greatest concentration of fish is in the upper reaches. Trout numbers lessen progressively from the Gray Reef area downstream to Casper due to the corresponding decline in the overall quality of trout habitat.

Over the past few years, many local fishermen have experienced a decline in the quality of fishing and have become resistant to more people coming to the area to fish. Local anglers adamantly believe too many fishermen are overharvesting this area. They resent the intrusion of out-of-state anglers, blaming them for the perceived degradation of the fishery. There has been a general decline in numbers and pounds of trout, even though there has been an increase in stocked numbers of trout. There has appeared to be a higher than normal harvest of trout by fishermen in 1989 and 1990, but this has only been a very small factor in the decline.

In 1987, a Continental Pipeline Company (subsidiary of Conoco, Inc.) pipe ruptured and sent about ninety thousand gallons of gasoline into the river at the mouth of Bolton Creek. An estimated 139,000 fish were killed in an eighteen-mile stretch of Blue Ribbon water, sixteen miles of Class II water, and five miles of Class III water downstream of the spill. Trout as large as fourteen pounds were found dead after the spill. Aquatic invertebrates were also killed. This devastation obviously affected the overall quality of fishing. Conoco did reach an agreement with the State of Wyoming to the tune of $332,520 that went to the Department of Fish and Game to be used for reimbursement for fish killed and restocking costs; expenses incurred during the spill and follow-up studies; the value of an eighty-three-acre parcel of land donated as a public fishing area and the development of this parcel.

Fish and game acted swiftly to attempt to restore the quality of fishing, and a rebound began. The aquatic invertebrates made a rapid recovery and the stocking program was increased, but the decline seemed to go on. Several factors are thought to have contributed to the reduced numbers of trout in the river since the spill. The major reason is probably the severe degradation of habitat due to the large amounts of sediment deposited into spawning and food-producing areas over the years. The drought conditions over these years have led to lower than normal flows, which have limited the flushing action of higher water.

The low, clear flows have enabled double-crested cormorants to feed heavily on stocked fingerlings. These birds have been on the increase for the past ten years and are now a major problem. They can be blamed for the poor survival of fin-clipped rainbow trout in low-flow years.

White pelicans have also become a problem, even though many biologists explain that these birds feed on slower-swimming species of fish, like suckers, rather than on the faster trout. Recently, Wyoming Fish and Game observed pelicans feeding at known rainbow trout feeding locations on this stretch. Several hundred of these birds fed heavily for most of April at these locations in 1990. Predation was thought to have been substantial. The combination of low flows, clear water, and unwary spawning rainbows made for excellent feeding conditions for the pelicans. It also made for excellent fishing conditions for fishermen, who did help in the harvest of fish. In years where there are turbid conditions, higher flows, or an early spawn, pelicans don't feed as heavily on these fish, even though they do return to the area.

Another factor that more than likely contributed to the decline in the quality of fishing was that the Eagle Lake strain of rainbow trout, which has been stocked in the river since 1985, does not survive as well as the strain that was stocked previously. Also, large numbers of fingerling rainbows that used to be stocked in Alcova Reservoir experienced a high mortality rate from predation by walleye. Many, however, would migrate downstream to below Gray Reef. These fish have been replaced with fewer but larger rainbows in an attempt to reduce the mortality rate in the reservoir. It appears that fewer of these bigger fish migrate downstream.

Even with these problems over the last few years, this is still an excellent fishery by any standard. With continued efforts by local clubs and agencies, this area will continue to rebound into a great fishery. For instance, 1991 had an excellent year-class of wild fish as proof of recovery.

Seasonal Changes in Fishing

Portions of this stretch of river are subjected to the traditional changes in seasons. The sections that are closer to Casper experience a winter freeze and a spring runoff. They endure the ravages of the weather, tending to get muddy when summer squalls dump sediment through tributaries. This stretch is also susceptible to the rise and drop in flows from the tailwater section upstream. Temperature changes are usually widely variable as the river nears Casper: more of the river is exposed to the warming sun in the summer and the freezing air in the winter.

The hatches downstream are more affected by seasonal changes than they are upstream, and so is the behavior of the fish. Water temperatures slowly rising toward the sixty-degree mark trigger feeding binges by the fish, and as it moves even higher, feeding urges are retarded. In some summer months the water may rise into the seventies, putting most fish down for the count in a semistressed condition. Because brown trout have a greater tolerance for warmer temperatures, this lower stretch is good brown trout water. The lower reach also has classic brown trout habitat, with slower, deeper runs.

The upstream tailwater is a more consistent fishery. Temperature changes occur on a gradual basis, slowly warming in the summer months and falling as slowly in the winter months. There is no runoff period in the spring and it does not freeze in the winter. Weather affects the river in only minor amounts, because most of the sediment-bearing tributaries are farther downstream. This is not to say that if a very severe thunderstorm should hit, the water will not murk up. It will to a small degree but will also clear quickly.

What does affect seasonal changes in the fishing upriver is the need for water by downstream irrigators in the spring and summer. This causes the flows to increase. In the fall and winter months the flows are reduced in order to store needed water in the upstream reservoirs, so the river then is generally low and clear. April and October are usually the months when the changes occur. The fishing immediately following a rapid change in flow is usually on the poor side until the fish have a chance to adapt. Because the Gray Reef Dam acts as an afterbay or regulatory dam, the water downstream runs at a pretty constant rate during its two seasons. The major fluctuations occur in the short span of river between the Alcova and Gray Reef dams.

The low, clear flows of the winter give way to higher, faster water in summer. When the flows are raised, the water tends to become turbid and stays on the turbid side throughout most of the summer, appearing greenish. After the fish have a chance to settle into the new flow, the murkiness does not seem to affect the way they feed, thus benefiting the fishing. Early in the spring there seems to be a period when there is a lot of moss in the drift; this certainly makes fishing difficult at best. The drifting moss does not allow the angler to get a good drift whether he is nymph-fishing, throwing a streamer, or dry-fly fishing. It catches on the line, leader, and fly, making for a frustrating experience.

Spring (March, April, and May)

The lower portion of this stretch of river is effectively shut down in the early part of spring with runoff or, in very cold years, it could still be partially frozen. The majority of fishing will take place in the upper tailwater, around Gray Reef. Midges dominate the top-water action in March, and pods of rising fish can be seen as one floats down the river.

It is extremely difficult to fish to trout taking midges if one is floating because the fish are usually feeding in quiet water with little current. To bring a boat into one of these areas would spook the fish, and to try to make a presentation to these fish from a boat floating in a faster current would be tough. Line control is difficult to achieve, and the fly almost always drags before it can be properly presented to the fish. An angler should get out of the boat to work these fish effectively. Drift by and well away from them, or, if you know where they are usually feeding, stop well above them and walk back to them. This can pose a problem if the property along the river is private, because you aren't supposed to get out of the boat in these places. I know it is common practice on this upper stretch of river to do so, but the proper thing to do in this situation is to pass on these fish or fish from the boat.

Traditional midge patterns and fishing techniques will take fish, but I think an adult and pupa two-fly setup is more effective. When one can fish from the bank, a soft-hackle cast to the faster currents and allowed to swing back to slower water in front of feeding fish is often very effective. A phenomenon unique to fish feeding on midges is that they seem to pod or school up and feed as a group in selected areas. One can float relatively long distances between these pods and not see other fish rising. In the latter part of the day, fish seem to spread out and take the occasional midge. These singletons can be found mostly in the tailouts of pools and runs.

Nymph-fishing is a far more consistent manner of taking fish in the spring and the rest of the year. Finding rising fish is a hit-or-miss proposition on this stretch of the river. There are times during a particular hatch when finding rising fish is very predictable but, for the most part, there are too many variables to take into account, such as bright sun and wind, to be positive about finding them. When I was trying to figure out what to use and when to use it here, I did a lot of kick-screening to see what was in the drift. Early spring finds the bottom of the river predominantly full of an olive caddis larva that could be matched on a #12, #14, or #16 hook. These are free-roaming larvae, not the cased variety, either a species of *Hydropsyche* or *Rhyacophila*, because some are quite green in color. A pattern tied specifically to imitate the caddis larva, an olive Hare's Ear, or a Bead Head Caddis Larva will work well.

Scuds are available in the upper sections of the tailwater, and a light rusty orange scud imitation is a local favorite. Most of the summer-hatching mayfly nymphs are still too small for trout to seek them out; there are a few more instars for them to go through. However, many of the early-hatching mayfly nymphs have reached a large enough size to interest the fish. I usually do fairly well with a #16 PMD nymph because it is a good general pattern and has the coloration of most of the scuds, but any nonspecific mayfly nymph pattern should be effective.

Somewhere from out of the twilight zone enters a fly that has been super effective at this time of year—the Halfback in #6, #4, and even #2. I have no clue what these big imitations represent because I haven't been able to find anything in the drift that comes close to resembling them. There are some stonefly nymphs in this section, but not in the same numbers as in other stretches.

The Halfback at times just knocks fish silly, and I really have no explanation for it on this section of river. Many fish are caught as the big fly swings in the current, so maybe it imitates a baitfish of some sort. All I know is that it does work when other patterns seem to fail.

There are some cranefly larvae (maybe the Halfback imitates them) in the drift, along with aquatic worms, but not in numbers sufficient to make fish key on them. Trout will take one occasionally as it drifts by, so patterns imitating the larvae should at least be tried.

Late March and early April is the season when a good deal of the rainbow trout will be spawning. Because rainbows are the dominant species in this stretch of river, some interesting action can be had, especially on known spawning grounds. Large, ugly, bright patterns will trigger strike reactions from these fish. Streamers will worry the rainbows into a protective strike and egg patterns always seem to produce. The moral dilemma of fishing over redds exists for some anglers. Streamer fishermen do pretty well at this time because some baitfish are also spawning and the fish seem to look for them. A pattern like the Red Head Streamer works well because it simulates the color of the spawning baitfish.

The middle of April brings high flows in some years as more water is released for downstream irrigation. It usually takes some time before the fishing is any good because the fish need to adjust to the flows, and the stronger water washes debris from exposed areas and the river bottom. Fish can still be caught but one must constantly clean moss from line and fly.

After this short, messy period subsides, the fishing picks up in full force. Insects other than midges begin to hatch, and others are getting ready to hatch. A brown-bodied mayfly with gray wings makes its appearance at this time. I believe it to be a *Paraleptophlebia* species, a red quill or slate-winged mahogany. The duns hatch out around noon and can be matched on a #16 hook. The nymphs of this mayfly swim to the slower water and crawl on anything that sticks out of the water about two inches above the water line. A #14 Hare's Ear swung into this slower water or very slowly retrieved through it will catch fish.

Blue-winged olives, *Baetis* species, also make their appearance, to the delight of many dry-fly fishermen. Fish feeding on these insects can very often be mistaken for midging fish because the behavior is similar. Pods of feeding fish will be found eating BWOs, as they do midges, but more fish will be found at the edges of riffles and in slightly faster water. Bank-feeding fish will also be spotted by the floating fisherman. Along the inside bends of riffles is a good place to look for fish because these insects hatch out of riffled areas. Later in the day, look to the banks along glides for fish holding tight and feeding. The riseforms are so slight as to be almost imperceptible, so pay attention.

After the spawn and into May, the male rainbow trout seem to herd in the tailouts and hang together. I've noticed this on many other rivers, so it must be part of their normal after-spawn behavior. Any large fly swung in front of these fish will almost always be ravaged because the trout are very aggressive now.

By the end of May the weather is nice and the summer season begins. Hatches become more plentiful and the overall fishing picks up. Caddis begin to make an appearance, as do the yellow sallys. The mayfly nymphs have mostly matured, so nymph-fishing is varied and consistent.

Summer (June, July, and August)

The lazy, hazy days of summer bring the kind of fishing that more traditionally resembles what most people think of as fly fishing: wait for a hatch, fish it, go home. Caddisflies dominate the early part of summer on riffled pieces of water. A floating fisherman can have tons of fun hitting the riffles, even on private property. He can put into the slack water on the inside bend of the riffle and work it without too much maneuvering to stay in position. Presentations can be made without too much concern for technique, especially if one uses an adult-emerger setup. On public land the wading fisherman can have success by methodically working the riffles from top to bottom.

Evening swarms of egg-laying caddis provide sport for the angler. This is mostly confined to the walking fisherman or one on a very short float.

Baetis are still around for the mayfly enthusiast, and so are the red quills. A smattering of other species hatch but not in sufficient numbers to be considered major. There may be areas of the river where concentrations of a particular mayfly might entice fish to feed, but this is not usually the case. An occasional green drake or gray drake may drift by in the late morning, as well as the occasional brown drake in the evening, or it may pay to prospect with a large dun pattern. PMDs begin to make an appearance on the surface, but the hatch doesn't get going until a little later in the summer.

The nymph fishing is excellent at this time. With so much maturing on the bottom of the river, there is a cornucopia of larvae for the fish to select from. Mayfly nymphs of many varieties, caddis larvae, little yellow sally nymphs, and other aquatic life-forms complete the menu for the fish, who may key on the special of the day but rarely pass up a properly presented morsel. A Red Fox Squirrel Nymph in #14 is very effective as an all-around searching pattern. It can suggest the mayfly nymphs that abound, and it does a good job imitating many of the caddis larvae found in the river. A friend of mine has success using a strip nymph in various sizes in a natural hare's ear color or tan. The old Halfback is still a consistent fish-taker.

July brings the best of the hatches when the PMDs and the yellow sallys get going. The PMD hatch on this section of river is one of the more predictable. An angler can nymph-fish in the morning, make the transition to duns with an emerger pattern, fish the adult stages, and then hit the spinner fall.

Once, while kick-screening, I happened upon PMD nymphs that were emerging from their nymphal shucks. The nymphs that were ready to burst free seemed to be darker, with a very shiny appearance. My partner, Steve, developed a flashback PMD nymph called the Electric Rabbit to imitate this stage and has had good success with it. Otherwise I use my PMD pattern in a #16 and do well. Often fish can be caught at one's feet when they are feeding heavily on this stage. Inside bends of runs and riffles are a great place to cast with a high-stick technique. We did this on a few occasions and had hooked rainbows jump straight out of the water a foot away from us.

An overcast, almost drizzly day will bring a strong PMD hatch on the river. The river seems to come alive with rising fish, but if you are floating, stop at a group of risers and fish them until you have your fill before you move on. Never leave rising fish, because they may be the last you see for the day.

Summer evenings will bring a PMD spinner fall that can be fished with a #14 Rusty Spinner. The slower current edges, tailouts, and bank sides are good places to fish the spentwings because the fish do not want to work very hard for a meal. Late afternoons and evenings can also see some spotty pale evening dun activity. Areas of this section of river have a fair hatch that is often overlooked because of the caddis or yellow sally activity. It is a relatively tough hatch to fish because fish that appear to be rising to duns are probably taking emerging duns—it is difficult to distinguish between the different riseforms. If you suspect the fish to be taking emergers, a soft-hackled pattern much like a flymph will probably be more effective than a dun. Fish it as you would a dry, with no drag and in the feeding lane.

By the time August rolls around, Tricos have made their initial appearance. The hatch here is not as spectacular as on the upper river, but it does occur and it can be fished. One of the problems encountered

Fishing the channels.

on this section is that many places where the Tricos hatch are between access spots, so unless one is on the water very early the hatch will go undetected. And very often the wind will interfere with the spinner fall. The huge swarms of Tricos that are very evident upriver may be blown apart by the time a floating angler reaches them in this section. Nevertheless, there are Tricos here and fish can be spotted feeding on the spentwings in the calm slow shallows. The Tricos seem to be a larger variety than the ones upriver, so #18 and #20 patterns work fine.

Terrestrials become somewhat important at this time of year. These land-based insects have become mature and abundant and very often get blown into the river. It happens with enough regularity over the course of the summer that some fish have learned to look to the banks for them. A well-placed beetle pattern will take a surprising number of fish in carefully selected areas. Banks that have vegetation close to the water's edge are decent spots for the beetle because many will blow off of the vegetation into the water. Some fish keyed to a mayfly will very often take a beetle pattern without hesitation. I have experienced times when I could not buy a fish, but when I switched to a #18 black beetle I did well. A tiny tuft of fluorescent yarn makes this fly infinitely easier to spot on the water.

The phenomenon of ants swarming is something that can frustrate an angler if he isn't observant. Very often, flying ants will swarm and the wind will blow them into the water in sufficient numbers to start pods of fish working as if they were feeding on a hatch. I have experienced this and been tricked by it, because I searched the surface for floating duns, finding none. I have then tried different mayfly patterns, thinking I must not be seeing them on the surface or in the air, with very spotty results. It was only after I took the time to carefully observe the feeding fish that I noticed the massive amounts of flying ants in the drift. I watched fish quietly sip these terrestrials off the surface. After I switched to an ant pattern I began taking fish with regularity. Even if ants aren't swarming, an ant imitation is often an effective prospecting pattern and may do the job on those fish sporadically feeding along the banks.

Grasshoppers are very abundant in certain years, and are an excellent food for trout. Much of this section of river flows through fields where hoppers are plentiful. Early afternoons are very often windy, and many hoppers get blown into the water, where some fish lie in wait for them. The hopper fishing is not as great here as it is on other rivers; perhaps the bank cover isn't as great here. Float in the current, throwing hopper patterns to any available cover along the banks, and wait for some savage strikes. The smaller low-water patterns seem to work best on this section of the river. Try adding some rubber legs to a low-water pattern as an added enticement.

Fall (September, October, and November)

The morning and evening hours begin to get crisper and the daylight doesn't last as long now. This is the time of year when many Wyoming sportsmen begin to think of hunting, so some of the pressure on the river begins to lighten up. The number of after-work floats taper down as the days shorten, and the recreational floats give way to other activities. Although weekends still see a good deal of pressure on the river, it does seem to ease up at this time. If one can get out on a weekday to fish, there is very little pressure.

The summertime hatches begin to wane in September as the fall insect activity increases. Caddis are still available, and there are some remnants of the Trico hatch. *Baetis* begin to emerge in greater and greater numbers, at least until it gets too cold or the water freezes in the downstream sections. The nymph fishing begins to really get going, and the fishing in general is very good. As the weather makes a turn to the colder and nastier, the only top-water action are the BWOs and some caddis.

Early in the fall, evenings can be spent fishing the egg-laying caddis with an adult and diving caddis imitation. There does seem to be a late-afternoon emergence of caddis in some of the riffles, but this will be a case of being at the right riffle at the right time.

Into the fall, the caddis action begins to taper off and the *Baetis* takes over as the major insect on the surface. They begin hatching in the late morning, but as the season progresses and the weather gets cooler, they hatch later and later in the day, probably as it takes longer and longer for the water to warm. The upper tailwater section has water that is of fairly consistent temperature, so this hatch is not as evident there. It's the lower sections that see the later hatches.

The fishing remains excellent in the upper section. As a matter of fact, it remains good all year long. But the autumn brings heavy feeding by the fish as they prepare for the cold, lean winter months. The lower stretch will see brown trout activity begin to accelerate. This is a good time to fish the lower stretch because of the browns' activity as they prepare to spawn. Many will stack up in the deeper water of runs after the first few really nasty days of October. Why they do this I haven't yet figured out. Almost all the fish caught in spots like this are males that will be breeding in the next few weeks or so. When the weather turns overcast and really cools down, some sort of trigger sets these fish off and they begin to stack up, offering excellent sport to the nymph and streamer fisherman. Keeping a fly down where these fish are is the key to success at this time. Popular streamer patterns include Woolly Buggers in black and olive, and Platte River Special variations. If the weather begins to get nice again, these fish disburse.

The middle of October is the traditional time when the river water is shut down to the winter flows. This can make fishing a little slow for a few days as the fish scurry for holding water where they feel confident and safe. After the flow adjustment is made, they begin to feed again. For the angler who wants a large fish, this is the time to try the lower section of the river. There is some very good brown trout habitat here, and the browns have begun to feed differently than they do at other times of the year. Their usual feeding habits give way to a more careless approach.

"Throwing heads" is a term the big-fish hunter uses to describe the streamer technique used at this time. These anglers use a heavy rod capable of casting a 7-, 8-, or 9-weight line and a streamer. The lines are heavy shooting heads attached to a running line. Very often the rods are overlined by one weight because during the cast the heavy shooting head can pull more running line out for greater distance. The objective of the long casts is to cover a great deal of water, and the objective of the very fast sinking head is to get the fly on the bottom, where the big fish lie. The type of water fished is the slow, deep pools at the ends of runs. The line and streamer should swing into the pool and be worked back along the bottom or presented broadside to the upstream-facing fish as it swings through the pool. It is a technique very much like the one a steelheading angler uses. Some amazing browns are taken by it.

November sees the browns spawning, and the fishing in the lower section begins to taper off. Most anglers will start concentrating on the upper tailwater section for the remainder of the year. The surface will see midges as the *Baetis* fall off. Most of the consistent fishing will take place beneath the surface. The nymph or streamer fisherman will begin working the water in earnest on the nicer days. The weather can turn brutal in November as winter approaches, so floating anglers need to take precautions in the form of extra warm, dry clothing at this time of year. A dunking can bring a case of severe hypothermia to the ill-prepared.

Winter (December, January, and February)

The angler who likes to fish in relative solitude can do so at this time of year, especially during the weekdays. This tailwater offers the winter angler fishing that is almost on a par with the Miracle Mile. The difference is that more smaller fish will be taken, and certainly more rainbows. The water flows have been turned down, so low, clear water is the norm. This is the time of year to leave the boat at home and walk the river. A boating accident can have severe consequences in the winter, and if the weather should happen to take a turn to the wild side while you are on the water, it could be a tough, miserable float to the take-out.

Those who do go out in the cold will find midges the dominant top-water insect. There is a little brown stonefly that hatches in the winter, though not in sufficient numbers to cause major feeding. This insect looks like a small brown caddis except for the wing shape and can often be seen on streamside vegetation. A brown bucktail caddis pattern will take the occasional fish when these insects are observed.

Nymphing is the way to be successful in the winter. Caddis larvae appear in good numbers, scuds are available, and there are other insects that become trout food. Nymphing remains good throughout the winter. February brings many of the larger rainbows into the areas one would normally nymph-fish as they begin to stack up and think of spawning. February is a good time for large fish.

Locally Effective Patterns

Caddis Larva

Hook:	12, 14, 16
Thread:	Brown
Ribbing:	Gold wire
Abdomen:	Light hare's ear or olive dubbing
Thorax:	Dark hare's ear dubbing
Legs:	Fibers from a partridge feather

Strip Nymph

Hook:	8-14
Thread:	To match fur
Tail:	1/16- to 1/8-inch-wide strip of hide with fur
Abdomen:	Dubbed fur from same hide
Wingcase:	Peacock herl pulled over the thorax
Thorax:	Guard hairs from same hide in a dubbing loop spun to make a chenille

Pale Evening Dun Flymph

Hook: 14, 16
Thread: Tan
Tail: Light brown partridge
            hackle fibers
Body: Light hare's ear dubbing
Hackle: Light brown partridge
            soft-hackle

Electric Rabbit

Hook: 12-18
Thread: Olive
Ribbing: Clear Antron fibers
Abdomen: 60% dark hare's ear and
            40% olive dubbing
Wingcase: Silver Mylar pulled over
            thorax
Thorax: Same as abdomen, picked
            out for legs

Pale Morning Dun Thorax

Hook: 12-18
Thread: Light gray
Tails: Medium blue dun Micro
            Fibetts, split and divided
Wing: Light blue dun hen hackle
            fibers bunched and upright,
            tied in at the middle of
            hook shank
Body: Pale sulphur or yellowish
            green dubbing
Hackle: Light blue dun hackle clipped
            in a vee in the bottom

Red Head Streamer

Hook: 2-10
Thread: Red
Body: Fine brown or yellow
            chenille, or none
Wing: Two yellow inside two
            brown hackles
Hackle: Red, as a collar

Red Quill

Hook: 12-18
Tails: Brown hackle fibers
Body: Natural red-brown hackle
         stem
Wing: Gray Z-lon, single tuft
Hackle: Brown

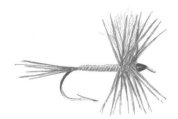

Other Effective Patterns

Scuds (rusty orange, olive)
Black Soft-Hackle
Little Yellow Stonefly Nymph
Yellow Sally
Palomino Midge (adult, pupa)
Midge larva
Griffith's Gnat
PMD
Rusty Spinner
Gold-Ribbed Hare's Ear
Halfback
Cranefly larva
San Juan Worm
Red Fox Squirrel Nymph
Caddis larva
Caddis emergent pupa

Diving caddis
Elk Hair Caddis
Bucktail caddis
Prince Nymph
Brassie
Blue Dun
Blue-Winged Olive
Baetis emerger
Adams
Pale Evening Dun
Glo-Bug
Nuclear Egg
Platte River Special (variations)
Woolly Bugger (black, olive)
Clouser's Deep Minnow

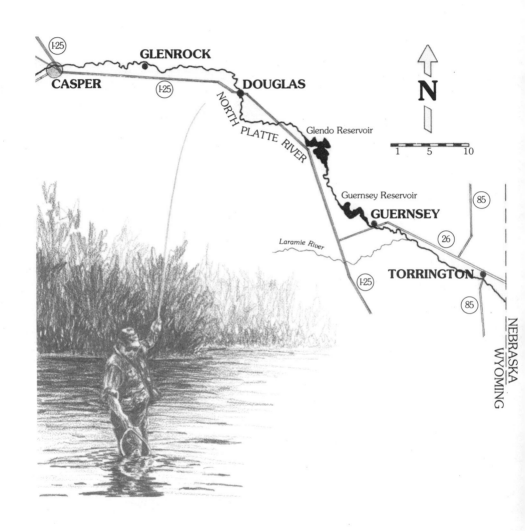

CASPER

GLENROCK

DOUGLAS

NORTH PLATTE RIVER

Glendo Reservoir

Guernsey Reservoir

GUERNSEY

Laramie River

TORRINGTON

N

1   5   10

NEBRASKA
WYOMING

10

Casper to Nebraska

As the North Platte makes its eastward journey away from Casper it becomes "just another river," and is nothing special in the way of trout fishing. The best water is classified as Class III (described as "important trout waters—fisheries of regional importance") and accounts for approximately twenty-five percent of the remaining river in the state. About half of the rest of the water is classified as Class IV, "low production waters—fisheries frequently of local importance, but generally incapable of sustaining substantial fishing pressure," and the other half is Class V, "very low production waters—often incapable of sustaining a trout fishery." There are approximately 150 miles of river in this stretch, but the avid trout fisherman will find very little water to fish in the traditional sense, especially when compared to the river upstream. This isn't to say there aren't trout in this section or decent fishing can't be had, because in some places under certain conditions some very good fish may be caught. But it is a matter of tailoring one's expectations to meet the conditions.

This section of river has become a warm-water fishery where channel catfish, walleye, perch, and carp may be caught. There are trout in parts of the river; some are part of a regular stocking program, some are dumped as excess fish, and some are planted strictly as a put-and-take proposition. Mostly these fish are brown trout, with a few individuals surviving to become very large. But the bulk of the water is anything but a trout fishery. There are many reasons for the decline in quality, but poor habitat and wild water-temperature swings are probably the most significant.

Along the river's course are two large reservoirs, Glendo and Guernsey. One would think, based on the excellent tailwater fisheries upstream, that these reservoirs would offer a similar experience to the angler, but this is not the case.

Casper to Glendo Reservoir

Let's break this 150 miles of river into three sections and take a look at some of the minimal possibilities for the trout fisherman. The first section is Casper to Glendo Reservoir.

The first third of this section is a Class III stretch and has stocked brown trout as well as channel cats. There are some access sites but no map because plans are in transition for the possible addition of more access areas. A call to the Casper office of Wyoming Fish and Game should provide information for the angler intent on fishing this area. Much of the river flows through private land, but permission to pass through may be granted if one were to approach the landowner and ask.

If an angler can get on this water to fly fish and concentrates on catching the browns that reside in this section, he might be surprised to see the good-sized football-shaped fish that are occasionally taken. Much of the fishing will be limited to subsurface presentations—streamers and large nymphs worked through the deeper water. There may be odd areas where trout will bunch up and feed on the surface if there is a hatch, and an occasional trout might be seen taking something off the surface through this section, but the character of the water doesn't lend itself to the classic forms of trout activity.

As we move downstream to the Douglas area, the river goes through a classification change to Class IV water just downstream of Glenrock. Sections of this stretch have undergone some river rehabilitation work, and the town of Douglas has had boulders placed for cover, but the stretch remains a Class IV water. Fish and game does plant catchables in the Douglas area in the spring and fall, but these are put-and-take fish. Brood-stock culls are planted in the town area, where the boulder placement provides some habitat. These culls are usually fish of three to four pounds and are also put-and-take. Just when these trout are planted the fishing can be hot and heavy, but it is short-lived. I suppose some fish do survive the intense fishing and grow to large proportions by feeding on the warm-water fish, but they are few. I would look for those fish to run upstream to the slightly better habitat.

The river in Douglas.

Downstream of Douglas the water is very marginal trout habitat because the water temperatures will quite often rise into the eighties, killing most or all of the trout population. The summer will find this section of the river discolored because of upstream water releases for the irrigators and sediment washed into the river from tributaries, particularly after a rain. If an angler wanted to fish the river with thoughts of catching a walleye, this would be a good stretch because they very often run up the river from Glendo Reservoir.

Glendo to Guernsey Reservoir

The water below Glendo to Guernsey Reservoir is Class III water with a marginal tailwater fishery. It looks on a map as if it should be a super fishery. It resembles the conditions found at the Miracle Mile in that it starts at the outflow of one reservoir and dumps into another. But there are two major differences: water temperature and water flow. Water temperatures will often reach into the seventies in this section

and every so often will hit the eighties, making it tough for trout to survive. Water levels and flows are extreme, from a mere trickle to very
high flow. Fish and game does hope that a good fishery can be established in the upper few miles in the future, and has plans to implement
this. One of the more serious problems is that, immediately below
Glendo, no water runs for six months out of the year. Actually, some
water seeps out of the dam, but only around 5 cfs. A friend of mine,
figuring he'd discover an underfished tailwater, attempted to fish there,
and although he didn't catch anything he did see some huge fish cruising
the pools below him. The possibilities are there for an excellent fishery
and only time will tell if it actually happens.

Access is poor on this stretch, but many of the landowners are fairly
good about allowing access, at least until too many people take advantage of their hospitality. A float trip from the base of Glendo Dam to the
intake at Guernsey is about eighteen miles and flows through Wendover
Canyon, but during low water this trip can take a couple of days. Private
land access, when found, can make floating this section more practical.
When the water is high and the flows are strong, float trips will obviously
take less time, but then it is practically impossible to fly-fish.

There are some trout planted in this stretch—it is used mainly as
a dumping ground for surplus fish. The good news is that a lot of these
fish survive and grow up to be wall-hanger size. Locally, this area is
known as a trophy fishery, and many brown trout better than eight
pounds are caught each year. It is not heavily populated with these huge
fish, and they are hard to come by—not only because trophy fish are
inherently finicky and difficult to catch, but because of the nature of
the water. When there are high flows it is almost impossible to fish, but
when there are low flows the river breaks up into large, almost currentless pools very much like big beaver ponds. This obviously makes things
tough on the average fly fisher. The angler with the patience and the
perseverance to systematically fish the beaver-pond-like pools can come
away with the fish of a lifetime. October is usually the best time to fish
for these lunkers as the fish put on the feed bag in preparation for the
long winter months ahead. Throwing heads would be a highly effective
way to work these pools with large baitfish imitations. Putting the fly
on the bottom where the large fish cruise should result in a bragging-
sized brown trout.

Guernsey Dam to the Nebraska Border

The river below Guernsey Reservoir.

The water from Guernsey Dam downstream to the Nebraska border is classified as Class V water, the poorest in the state. Habitat is really poor and there are virtually no flows from the dam to where the Laramie River meets the North Platte for six months out of the year. December is virtually bone dry. There is a minimum flow from the Laramie River as it flows out of Gray Rocks Reservoir into the main river, but it has a shifting sand bottom that makes for poor trout habitat. This area is not considered a viable trout fishery. There are plans to stock one thousand catchable rainbow trout a year in Torrington as put-and-take fishing in the fall, when the flows for irrigation calls drop.

This stretch of river is not a section that will ever become a destination for the trout fisher. It is more or less a local fishery: those who live nearby will know where and when to fish for best results. It would be a tough section for the visiting angler to get a handle on, especially on a short trip.

Before the river makes its exit from the state it dies a quiet death as a trout fishery. It slowly degenerates until it passes away without fanfare.

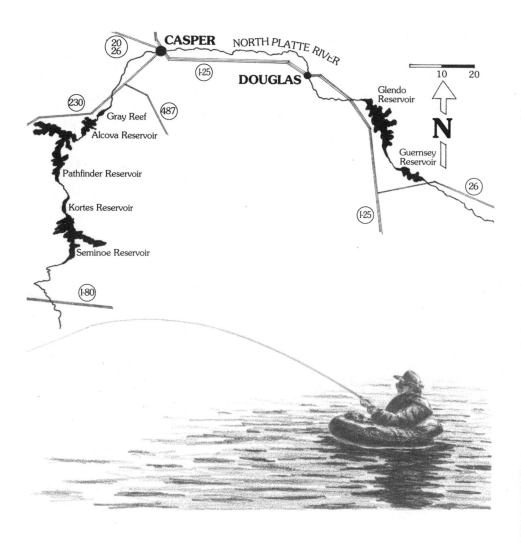

CASPER

NORTH PLATTE RIVER

20
26

I-25

230

487

DOUGLAS

Gray Reef

Alcova Reservoir

Pathfinder Reservoir

Kortes Reservoir

Seminoe Reservoir

I-80

Glendo
Reservoir

Guernsey
Reservoir

26

I-25

10   20

N

11

Reservoirs

The North Platte flows through some substantial reservoirs on its down-stream journey. There are five large impoundments: Seminoe, Path-finder, Alcova, Glendo, and Guernsey; and two smaller ones: Kortes and Gray Reef. All are viable trout fisheries with the exception of Glendo and Guernsey, which contain mostly warm-water species.

There are some fly-fishing opportunities on these reservoirs, but they are limited in scope. At certain times of the year fishing can be excel-lent and just a tad dangerous. Most of the impoundments, with the exception of Kortes and Gray Reef, are large and set in wide-open areas where the wind often howls. The water can be whipped to a froth in a very short period, causing some acute adrenalin surges in the float-tuber or small-craft operator. When the wind does blow, a float-tubing angler may not have the kick to combat it and might find himself blown across the water. Many a small-boat operator has had bouts with hypo-thermia after a soaking in the wind-whipped waves. Caution and a serious eye on the weather are suggested when an angler is out on one of these impoundments.

All the reservoirs have healthy populations of rainbow trout of various strains. The Eagle Lake and Kamloops strains are very popular in stock-ing programs. Brown trout and cutthroats are also residents. A number of years ago, fish and game stocked a strain of brown trout, the Ohrid, in Pathfinder Reservoir because it is supposedly capable of reproduc-ing in a still-water environment. These fish have now become wild and self-sustaining.

Reservoirs with viable spawning areas upstream have populations of wild fish that return to the reservoir after spawning. Most of the rainbows that have been planted are lake-oriented, prefer a large still-water environment, and spend most of their lives there, but they will make upstream spawning runs and return to the reservoir. Obviously, most of the reservoirs are primarily rainbow fisheries.

Some of the reservoirs have very healthy populations of walleye, which have caused major problems in the attempt to manage the impoundments as trout fisheries. The most significant problem has been predation on stocked trout by the walleye. It took years of trial and error before fish and game figured out that a stocked trout had to be a little longer than half the length of the average-sized walleye to have any chance of survival. Once this was worked out, trout populations began to increase, but a problem still existed: the larger trout and walleye began to compete for the same food sources. As I understand it, Seminoe Reservoir was, at one point in time, a super brown trout fishery and grew many large fish. When walleye were introduced, the populations of larger brown trout rapidly declined to where there are currently few large browns left. The large browns' primary food source was the crawfish, which were found in good numbers in the reservoir. Apparently, the increasing numbers of walleye were more efficient at feeding on the crawfish and depleted them to the point where it was tough for a large brown to survive. Attempts are being made to establish other food sources in the reservoirs.

Most of the reservoirs share the same problem that inhibits the growth of trout after a certain point and indirectly inhibits the fly-fishing possibilities. The establishment of healthy weed beds is severely checked by fluctuating water levels. As water is stored for future use the levels rise, but when the irrigation season arrives water is released and the levels drop, sometimes drastically. Near-drought conditions have caused the water levels to reach all-time lows. The weeds that would normally grow in the shallower areas of relatively stable lakes and become food factories, allowing multitudes of insects to establish themselves, are not given the chance to get started in the reservoirs. If they begin to grow when the water is high, the dewatering leaves them dry and dying. If they begin to grow when the water is low, the increasing levels cover them with too much water, cutting off the sunlight necessary to sustain them. Without these weed beds, the fly fisherman will find limited fishing opportunities over a barren bottom.

A variety of insect life is necessary for trout to feed on in order to reach large sizes. A myriad of insect life and billions of crustaceans make a rich diet that grows some monster fish. Without established food-producing weed beds, trout have to look elsewhere for nourishment. In many of the reservoirs, the trout feed on tiny planktonlike organisms by trapping them in their gill rakers. But once these fish reach a certain size, the spaces in the gill rakers become too wide, making efficient feeding a real problem. At the same time, when they reach a length of around sixteen inches trout become predaceous and need a good supply of baitfish or other large food items to maintain growth. The limited supply of large food items in some of the reservoirs has prevented trout from reaching trophy weights and lengths. There are very few trophy fish in the reservoirs at the moment.

Attempts to establish different self-sustaining species of baitfish are currently being made. It seems the emerald shiner is taking hold in many of the reservoirs. This baitfish was originally only found in Lake Superior. If baitfish populations could ever reach a level where they are plentiful enough to survive the ravages of the walleye, trout will have the opportunity to attain trophy proportions, making fishing that much more exciting.

Kortes Reservoir is a case in point. This little riverlike reservoir has a population of fish that have drifted into it from the outflow of Seminoe. It's in a canyonlike setting with steep walls—the closest thing to wilderness fishing in the area, and it has almost no weed growth. A study done ten years ago showed mice that had fallen into the water from the steep canyon sides were the dominant food source in netted brown trout. A more recent study found no mice in the diet but showed the emerald shiner was the dominant food source.

The lack of weeds and accompanying insects in the reservoirs makes for limited fly-fishing opportunities. With no damselfly nymphs, scuds, *Callibaetis*, or midges to imitate, the fly fisher is forced to attempt to match the food sources that are available to the fish. That may be limited to baitfish imitations and some crawfish patterns. Without the weed beds to keep fish concentrated, the angler will be fishing mostly to cruising fish. This can be a hit-or-miss proposition.

Immediately after ice-out in the spring is a very good time to fish. The trout seem to cruise the shallower water near the shore looking for a meal—maybe this is the time when the baitfish attempt to spawn. The fly fisher in a float tube or small boat (I've even seen anglers in canoes) can reach these fish with streamer patterns and have great success. A slow- to medium-density line or a sinking tip is generally needed to get the pattern below the surface. It isn't necessary to reach great depths at this time because the trout are cruising in the shallows. A slow trolling or drifting with the breeze will take fish, as will a stripping retrieve. Fish will often be taken very close to the boat or tube as an angler begins to lift line out of the water.

The water is very cold at this time of year, and the float-tubing angler needs to be prepared with warm clothing under his waders. If the water is rough, stay off it; the cold water alone will sap energy from one's body, and the exertion of kicking back to shore against the wind can be hazardous to one's health. Ice-out is probably the time of year when the wading fly fisherman can be most effective because the fish are close to shore in good numbers.

As the season stretches into summer, it becomes difficult to consistently catch trout because the fish are more dispersed throughout the water. The wading angler will find fishing to be on the tough side. The angler using high-density, fast-sinking lines will take some fish by trolling streamer patterns from a float tube or boat.

Years ago, I used to vacation in the Moosehead Lake region of Maine, spending many summer hours fishing for brook trout, lake trout, and landlocked salmon. Deep trolling was the accepted way of fishing, but the technique was weird. We would use fly rods with large flylike reels containing lead-core or wire line. Streamers or baitfish were trolled behind sets of flashers, an array of huge spinners. The flash of the spinners was supposed to get the attention of the fish so they would take the streamer. These were ugly, unwieldy rigs that were hard to handle and made any hooked fish feel like an old dishrag. Some of the old-timers had fly rods with permanent sets or bends in them from constantly being doubled over by the weight of the trolling rigs. It was a very strange way to fish. The elimination of the gaudy flashers did not make too much of a difference to the fish, especially the landlocked salmon, as long as one could reach their depth. A lead-core line with a short leader ahead of a streamer was very effective when trolled at the proper depth. Lead-core lines changed colors every ten feet so an angler could gauge how deep he was. "Fish seven colors around that point," or something to that effect were common instructions to newcomers.

There are fly lines on the market that will sink very fast and can be trolled behind a slow-moving boat, but I don't think they can ever get as deep as lead-core line can. Fly lines are limited to certain depths because of the length—they are too short to get very deep. Lead-core lines can get deeper faster than any fly line I know of. I have never seen an angler using the trolling technique out here in the West. It hardly resembles fly fishing except that a fly rod is used. I bring it up only because of its interest to the angler who might appreciate traditional regional fishing practices. It is an old-fashioned approach to still-water fishing and probably still accounts for many fish taken in the Northeast. I don't see why it wouldn't work on large reservoirs. Give it a try for nostalgic reasons, or at least to see the expression on your partner's face when you pull out the equipment. And you just may catch some trout.

In the reservoirs with populations of crawfish, try working an imitation around rocky points and inclines. A relatively fast-sinking line is needed to get the fly down to the bottom. Use a fast, long stripping technique with frequent hesitations to imitate the erratic movement of the natural. Don't be too surprised if you happen to catch a walleye in the process.

Because there are no hatching insects, surface activity is very limited, but there is some. Land-based insects often get blown to the water's surface, especially in areas with high banks at the water's edge. There usually isn't any real vegetation at the edge of the water for insects to fall from, but fish have learned to look to the surface around the more windblown banks. They know that sooner or later something will end up in the water, so they cruise the area. Ants, particularly when they swarm, are the most common insect blown into the water. When a swarm gets blown onto the water a feeding frenzy takes place by waiting trout, often fooling the angler into thinking that a hatch is taking place.

Other insects find themselves swimming the reservoirs also. Make sure an extra spool with a floating line is part of your equipment because it is awfully tough to catch fish feeding on the surface with a sinking line. I tried it once. Ever attempt to put fly floatant on most of a sinking line? It doesn't work very well. Also, carry some ants whenever you fish one of these large still waters—you never know.

12

The Best of the River

"There's too much damned water, where do I go?" demanded a guy on the other end of my phone line one otherwise peaceful evening. I get a lot of calls similar to that; most are more polite, but all want information about where to go, when to go there, and what to use. I think it's called planning. Usually people want some general information, a "point me in the right direction and I'll take it from there" kind of thing, but occasionally a guy will grill me about specifics, including how I tie certain patterns. Local knowledge is usually good to have when planning a trip, especially when the river is as large as the North Platte and, at times, as finicky.

An interesting aspect of this river is that local fishermen are usually just that: they fish their local water and rarely venture to other sections. For as often as I fish the Miracle Mile, there have been only a few times when I have encountered anyone from the Saratoga area. Same with the Rochelle easement—anglers from Casper and Saratoga hardly ever fish it.

I believe an angler could spend the entire year fishing the North Platte and reasonably expect to have very good fishing if he knows when and where to go. Often the fishing is marginal on one section of water when it is excellent on other sections. Here, in my opinion, are the best times to fish the best places.

January

The Miracle Mile is my first choice: the opportunity to catch a really large fish exists, the fishing is generally good, and there are very few people to compete with. Of course, it can be awfully cold. My second choice is the Gray Reef area: the fish aren't quite as large, but they are acceptable, and the possibility does exist for a trophy (although the odds are better on the Mile). Both sections are limited to nymph-fishing, and a Rusty Orange Scud would be a good bet for constant action.

February

Again, the Miracle Mile is my first choice because of the large fish, but the fishing begins to taper off toward the end of the month. Some top-water midge activity becomes available and the crowds are still light. The same goes for the Gray Reef area. The Rusty Orange Scud is still a good bet for the nymph fisherman, and the Palomino Midge for the dry-fly fisherman.

March

This is an odd month because there are some other waters that open briefly. My first choice is still the Miracle Mile for the midge fishing, but this is only if the weather permits, or should I say the wind. When there is little or no wind the midge hatches are very good and so is the fishing. My experience is that the nymph-fishing is generally slow, but there are days when a Nuclear Egg pattern just slays fish. My second choice is the Gray Reef, which offers some decent nymph-fishing with scuds and Halfbacks. My third choice is any other water that is clear and fishable. The section near Rawlins can have clear water for a week or two with very good fishing, mostly for rainbows on stonefly nymph patterns. The Saratoga area can also see open and clear water with good fishing.

April

Another strange month that sees some waters open briefly. I like the Gray Reef area for the nymph-fishing and the opportunity to get in on some of the hatches of slate-winged mahoganies. The Miracle Mile, in my opinion, gets real finicky at this time—one day it fishes real well and the next it seems dead. Spawning rainbows might have something to do with that. The *Baetis* hatches can be quite good when the wind allows, and there are still some midges around. The nymph-fishing is somewhat slow, but it begins to pick up toward the end of the month. The crowds are starting to come back, especially on weekends with good weather. Most of the other waters are roiled with runoff, but there is a slight possibility of clear water in the Saratoga area.

May

My first choice early in the month is to fish the area upstream of Saratoga provided the water is clear—there can be excellent nymph-fishing. Later in the month it is a toss-up between floating the river up-stream of Saratoga or the headwaters section in North Park; both depend on water conditions. Woolly Buggers and big stuff provide the action. Those who don't mind crowds will find the Mile fishing very good with small mayfly nymphs and scuds; there will probably be some caddis action later in the month.

June

My first choice early in the month is to float the North Platte up-stream of the Encampment River and toss streamers and large nymphs to the banks. Treasure Island to town is not a bad bet throughout the month. Around the third week in June you will find me in the Encamp-ment River fishing the green drake hatch along with some of the caddis hatches. The caddis hatches above and below Saratoga are worth spend-ing some time fishing.

July

There are a lot of choices this month, but the section of river from Saratoga to Pick Bridge is hard to beat for the PMD hatches; the Gray Reef area comes close, and I do usually make a few trips there around midmonth. The Rochelle easement in the Rawlins area also has good hatches of PMDs. A trip or two to the Sixmile Gap area to fish the Trico hatches may be combined with an overnight campout. The Miracle Mile has some excellent fishing with wet flies and diving caddis patterns in the evening, when the caddis return to lay eggs.

August

To me August means Tricos, and my first choice is the Rochelle easement, where there are no people and super fishing. The Pick Bridge and Treasure Island areas also have some good Trico action.

September

This is one of the months when the fishing is good almost everywhere. The Mile is discolored, so I usually keep away from it. The Rochelle and Pick Bridge areas still have Tricos early in the month. Pick Bridge has good evening fishing with diving caddis patterns or wet flies, and the Rochelle easement begins to see very good numbers of *Baetis*. The Dugway area around Rawlins has a great white fly (*Ephoron*) hatch right before dark. The sections of river from Treasure Island to Saratoga and from Saratoga to Pick Bridge have excellent *Baetis* hatches.

October

There is good fishing everywhere, weather permitting. The Saratoga area can offer good action for brown trout with stonefly nymphs, and dry-fly action with the *Baetis* hatches. The Rawlins area around Carson's has good general fishing for cutthroats. If it's a big brown you're after, try the section of river from Government Bridge to Casper using streamers fished deep and slow, or try the Miracle Mile, although you will have to fight the crowds.

November

The nasty weather that usually hits now drives most of the fishermen away from the Mile, so I usually return there to fish seriously. There is good fishing with scud patterns for large fish. Most of the other sections of river, with the exception of Gray Reef, begin to ice over, or the water gets too cold to fish.

December

Look to the Miracle Mile and the Gray Reef section for open water, large fish, and very few people. The fishing is generally excellent until a spell of below-zero weather slows it down. Around Christmas there is a minor spawning run of rainbows on the Mile. If the weather doesn't get too nasty there are also good midge hatches.

Index